HOW TO HUNT A BEAR
By Revital Shiri-Horowitz

HOW TO HUNT A BEAR
By Revital Shiri-Horowitz

Editor: Shlomit Lica
Cover and interior design: Avner Haberfeld

Publishing House: Horowitz Publishing

All rights reserved, including the right to reproduce this book or portion thereof in any form whatever. For more information, please contact
revital@revitalsh.com

HOW TO HUNT A BEAR

By Revital Shiri-Horowitz

DEDICATION

Dedicated to the past and future generations of the extended Hauzer family, especially to my dear Uncle Ichu-Itzhak, who always made sure that the trip from his and my beloved Aunt Nurit's house to the local grocery store was enticing, who made riding around on his motorcycle was always a special adventure, and who always bought us large quantities of the most delicious pretzels. Writing this book has made me appreciate your optimism and zest for life even more than I already did.

Dedicated with love to Ofra Sofri, Ichu and Nurit's daughter, my oldest friend, who is only a year older than me, who has always accompanied my life journey, and vice versa.

Dedicated to my partner Amnon, to my children, and to my soon-to-be daughter-in-law.

Dedicated to the memory of all those who completed their life journeys during the war and to those who have carried it with them ever since.

Chapter One:
ICHU, SEPTEMBER 1939

TARNOBRZEG, POLAND

"Ichu, Ichu!" I barely heard my mother calling me. We had wandered far from home this time around.

"Shimon," I said to my older brother, "come, we need to go home." But Shimon didn't like stopping the game in the middle and always found a way to keep it going for a few more minutes. We jumped into a puddle, and mud splattered all over our clothing. We didn't mind, knowing it wouldn't make Mother angry. We made it home just in time for the Sabbath. Mother had already boiled hot water for our Shabbos bath. After we are scrubbed and bathed, Father will return from the synagogue, and we will gather with Grandpa, Grandma, and our uncles and aunts for dinner. I had already bought the cigarettes for Uncle Naphtali—two Polsky and one Ermeti. Three cigarettes a day, all of which he will manage to finish before the Sabbath. I prepared myself for my weekly discourse with Father over the Sabbath table. Soon enough, he would ask me questions about what I had learned in *cheder*[1] that week. I reviewed a long list in my head, making sure I was ready for the conversation. Hayke, Shloime's

---

[1] A traditional Jewish elementary school

mother, passed in front of us. She carried a warm loaf of bread, and we locked eyes, praying in our hearts that this week Mother may have enough money to buy us bread, and perhaps even a slaughtered chicken, to add to our Sabbath dinner table.

Next to the town square stood the Town Council House, where two giant flags decorated with swastikas were hung a few weeks ago. Nazi soldiers marched around the town square; their trucks parked all over the place. They looked at us and even smiled, but I felt uneasy whenever I saw them. I had heard things, such as the fact they aren't always nice to Jews. A few days ago, I heard my parents whispering that Shloime, from the Kollel, accidentally crossed their path. They beat him to the ground, stole his hat, and pulled his beard until they almost tore it off. Since then, he refused to come to the Kollel, or even to leave the house. I stared at Shimon, who looked away, as if to shield me from the fear in his eyes. On the last turn toward home, I saw a man in uniform. He had a swastika woven onto his sleeve. He approached Shimon, and my mother's words rang in my ears. I thought I had forgotten what she told me since I didn't like scary stories, but she wanted to warn me about the soldiers when she told me "Don't sneak any glances at them and walk quickly, as fast as possible, and get away from there."

I grasped Shimon's hand firmly as he whispered, "Walk quickly, as fast as you can. Yankale told me that Weisman's son was caught looking at the Germans, and they beat him up and cut off his sidelocks."

I looked at Shimon, my heart beating out of my chest and hoped that he had noticed who was walking in front of us, but Shimon was looking at Chayke passing by, and he almost bumped into the scary soldier. At the last second, I tugged on his hand, and he shifted his gaze to stare straight ahead. We tried to become both invisible and all-seeing. The soldier moved on, and we continued walking.

"Did you see that scary soldier?" I said to Simon breathlessly, but he snorted and replied, "What's scary about him? He's only wearing a uniform. He doesn't scare me one bit. I was just trying to scare you when I told you about Yankale. Do you want to tell me you'll believe anything that comes out of my mouth?"

I looked at him sternly, knowing that he had been telling the truth before, but now he was lying only so I wouldn't be afraid. I said nothing, and we continued walking.

When we got home, Mother rushed us to the bathtub, grumbling that we were even dirtier than we had been last Friday. But we were pleased by, and even proud of, the dirt we had accumulated. We handed her our clothing and soaked for an hour or so in the bathwater, which became lukewarm by the end of our scrub. Soon we sat at the Sabbath table, breathing comfortably, thanks to Grandpa Eli staying away from his cigarettes for the whole day. Grandpa Eli was funny, which was why I liked him the best out of all my grandparents. He was strong, even if sometimes things fell out of his hands. And out of everyone, he told the best bedtime stories. Grandpa Eli sewed at night and slept during the day—that is how my Grandpa Eli is.

I waited impatiently for my birthday. On Sukkot, I would have seven years under my belt, and Mother had already promised to make babka especially for me. Babka was my favorite cake—I could eat a whole half of it all by myself.

Chapter Two:
ITZHAK, DECEMBER 2018

JERUSALEM

More than eighty years have passed since then, and my eyes have long since stopped relishing the beauty of the world; my body is tired, most of the time even in pain, yet my mind is clear, and my memories are sharp. I was born in the small village of Tarnobrzeg, which sits on the Vistula River in Poland. It is safe to say that you have never heard of this infamous village. At the beginning of World War II, it was populated with around two thousand people, most of them Jews. Most of them were also poor and made a living from their artisanship, but the cultural and spiritual life of Jews and non-Jews alike was very rich. There were three religious study halls, three Jewish schools, libraries, and a sports center, as well as centers for Zionist youth movements, which held frequent meetings.

The town's Jewish community was unified. Holidays and festivals were celebrated proudly, and time passed idly, besides the few occasions on which I felt the Polish hatred toward me—but I was a young boy, and what did I know about hatred? Most of my extended family members—on both my father's and mother's sides—lived in the village, a few lived in the next village over, and two of my father's sisters had gone as far as Krakow. We lived on land belonging to my grandfather, Grandpa

Eli, my mother's father. Directly behind his house, they'd built a small structure for my parents, which we lived in for as long as we stayed in the village.

We shared a backyard with the extended family who lived nearest to us. My grandfather was a widely respected tailor, and while my father engaged in various crafts, what was certain was he had inherited his father's hands of gold. He knew how to build, repair, fortify, and even cultivate, fruit trees. He spent most of his days outside the house, while my mother raised their four young children, two boys and two girls: Shimon, Shifra, Sima, and me. We were close in age and to each other. We lived quiet, peaceful lives, full of family happenings, small and large, in a Jewish community that enjoyed a warm solidarity.

My full name is Itzhak, but I am mostly known as Ichu. I've lived for eighty-six years. That war is light-years away from my tiny room in a Jerusalem nursing home. My mind is clear, and the spirit of life still resides in me. My bodily pain only strengthens my spirit, reminding me of the gift that is time, and the importance of documentation—so I document, as is our duty, to ensure that the war and the Nazis are not forgotten long after their names and memories are erased. I am grateful for the gift of life that I have been given and for the old age that I have attained. I take none of it for granted.

When I decided to document my family story, I looked for a professional. I interviewed a few people, some of them highly experienced, but one in particular caught my attention. Her name was Maya, and she was clearly intrigued by my story. She said she usually held a party for her clients when she completed a project, inviting people from all stages of their life to attend. Her kind eyes, her earnestness, and the party she promised convinced me that I had found my match, so we began to work together. I tell her my story, and she types it furiously into her computer. I haven't seen any of it yet, but she assured me that I would be happy with the results, and I have faith in her.

Chapter Three: MAYA, 2018

TEL AVIV

I listened to the tape, to the questions that were posed, and the measured responses that were given. Glancing at the clock, I saw that there was still two hours until the kids' carpool home. Two whole hours. Should I keep going or leave the writing for tomorrow? The house was a mess. The beds weren't made, there were loads of laundry to do, and the refrigerator was empty, cleaned out even of leftovers. I had woken up overwhelmed by the list of things that awaited me to do in the next two hours. What day was today? For a moment, I panicked—let it be any day but Friday. I'd already forgotten a few times when there was a half-day at school, leaving my kids waiting to be picked up.

It was only Tuesday. I could relax. I passed through the rooms, picking up underwear, wet towels, socks strewn on the floor. I made the beds and swiftly tucked the sheets back into their corners, chucked the laundry basket down the stairs, ran down to retrieve it, and loaded the machine, all the while being trailed by the dog. In the process, I called my sister, who I hadn't spoken to in weeks, and who told me all about her stressful day at work. There wasn't even time to discuss getting together for coffee. We're both in way over our heads. I called my husband and asked how his day was going. He spoke in short sentences, signaling that he wasn't alone. I hung up and called my mom. She went into minute detail about her back trouble, before switching to the subject of her constipation. Too much information. She asked when I would bring her grandchildren for a visit, and I promised we'd come over the weekend.

When I hung up, I discovered that I'd already started the washing machine, diced some vegetables, and marinated several chicken breasts. I glanced at the clock, grabbed the car keys, and headed to the hallway. The sun's heat beat down on me, and it was hard to breathe, even though it was only the middle of April. I turned on the radio, then immediately turned it back off and put on some relaxing classical music. I tried to appreciate the serenity of the solo drive before picking up the kids.

For these few minutes of tranquility, I set aside politics, terrorist attacks, forest fires, and polarizing hatred. "I earned this," I whispered to myself. The kids were waiting for me outside the school. Apologizing for my lateness, I gave them each a bear hug and a kiss on the cheek. Avishay ignored my apology, got into the car in a huff, and declared that he "hates, but really really hates, the gym teacher who lets the girls play soccer but not the boys," while Dana retorted, "I actually really like the gym teacher, plus she's the prettiest teacher in the school."

I tried to calm Avishay down by asking him questions. "Avishay, what did the boys do while the girls were playing?" But this enraged him even more, and he said, "The boys got the basketball court in the auditorium, but everybody was fighting, and nobody could figure out who was on their team, and the teacher was busy with the girls and didn't even come help."

I smiled to myself, pleased that the day had finally arrived when girls were allowed to play soccer, and the gym teacher actually paid attention to them. I didn't say that, though, and focused on calming down my son, suggesting that he should talk to his gym teacher—whom I happened to really like, despite the overwhelming jealousy that her perfectly toned body induced in me—and ask her if maybe the girls and boys could play soccer together. But Avishay stopped me in the middle of my sentence and shouted, "You don't understand anything! Soccer is played with twenty-two players, not forty!"

I didn't respond, and in the meantime, Dana asked to stop for popsicles at Margalit's mini-market, and I agreed. When the three of us sat down, I felt as though our collective stress had settled, and I asked, "So, what else is new? What happened today at school? And what did you do during recess?"

While the kids chatted, my thoughts drifted to my chronic lack of sleep and to the hope that maybe tonight I would get in a few good hours. It had been weeks—ever since I embarked on the life story project—since I'd slept soundly. It is as if the war had never ended, and instead, had found a way to drip its insidious remains into my life.

One recent war has been with Yairi. Sometimes I wonder where the sweetheart I married has gone; life's burdens have taken a heavy toll on us. Tonight, he decided that Avishay must finish his homework for next week, a week early. Avishay explained that he had other plans, but Yairi, who is usually so calm and collected—so much so that I often ask him how it is that he never gets angry— was fuming. I took the girls to their room, then went back to the living room to try to quell the deafening shouts coming from Yairi and my son's heartbreaking tears.

Standing between the two of them, I said quietly, "Avishay, go to your room, I'll come soon."

Yairi was so surprised by my reaction that he stopped himself and looked at me with a broken expression, the kind I'd seen only once or twice during our marriage. "Don't you dare do that again," he said. "Don't you dare get between me and Avishay. I want the best for him just as much as you do."

Turning my back to him, I said, "This child doesn't belong to either of us. He belongs to himself." Tears welled up in my eyes. I went to Avishay's room, where he was still whimpering, and explained that Aba was angry and that he'd eventually calm down, but inside I wondered what in the world was going on. After Avishay felt better and everybody had gone to sleep, I went over to Yairi's desk and sat on the green couch that we'd picked out together when he landed his first job at TTE. The room used to be his study, but now it was more of a playroom, with his desk crammed into the corner.

When Yairi noticed me, he stopped staring at the computer, turned to me, and said, "Avishay drives me crazy. I refuse to accept his irresponsibility. He needs to learn to hold himself accountable, and you're not teaching him, so I will."

I could barely believe the iciness that emerged from his eyes, which I'd seen only when he spoke to strangers who had ticked him off. I froze, then got up and left the room without a word; there was no point. I went to the girls' room and then to Avishay's, turned off the light that was still on, stroked his hair, and tiptoed out. I recalled the day he was born, how overjoyed his father and I had been at the sight of such a miracle that had just emerged from my belly, how we'd stroked him, how Yairi's eyes had lit up, how much I loved him in those moments. I went to bed with a dark, heavy sorrow consuming me.

I lay awake in bed for a long hour. I thought about the years that had passed—the last one in particular—and wondered what had happened to the peaceful person with whom I had fallen in love. An impatient, intolerant man had grown inside of him, crowding out the old Yair, and I was no longer able to bring him back. I've tried so many times and in so many ways, but in vain. I'm lucky to be so busy with the kids and with my work. Every project I receive is a world unto itself, and the people I interact with frequently become like family to me. Like Itzhak. I'm so happy that he chose me to tell his story. When we first met, I felt an immediate connection between us; his story is so different from the other Holocaust stories I've heard.

When I started to write, I hadn't known much about the pre-war Eastern Polish Jewish community, let alone the history of their exile to Russia. I didn't know how trying the lives of people who survived the war inside Russia had been, how horrible the war had been for them, how they hadn't been recognized as Holocaust survivors because of never having been in the camps. But they survived a treacherous, painful journey, and for a long time, they knew nothing but starvation, freezing temperatures, and loss.

For a few minutes, I distracted myself from what was happening at home, but when Yairi came to bed, I tried to steer him back to the confrontation with Avishay. Turning away from me, he said that he was tired, and that all he wanted was to go to sleep.

"Just leave it for now, Maya, I don't have the energy to discuss it," he said.

Before I could protest his unwillingness to work through the difficult evening, he fell asleep. I lay in bed, trying to think through what had happened over and over again. I felt a hole in my heart; the same hole I had discovered one day when I was a little girl. But there wasn't truly any connection between that sorrow and the one I was currently facing. A small raincloud floated above me, reminding me that I was no longer the helpless girl I had once been; if I didn't like Yairi's behavior, I had to find a way to discuss it with him and solve the problem.

When I finally fell asleep, it was a fitful one, with people marching in file through my dreams, wearing threadbare clothing, carrying nothing, and I was marching together with them and with my children, but without Yairi. He wasn't there. We searched for him, but a torrential downpour began, and a Nazi shouted something in German that I didn't understand. And I knew that if I didn't save Yairi, I would lose him forever. I tried to say something to the Nazi, but to my surprise in the Yiddish that I'd learned from Grandma Matilda, words I didn't know I even remembered. He pushed me forward, and I almost stumbled, but I was able to keep my balance and kept walking. When I awoke from the bad dream, my pulse throbbed, and I was bathed in a cold sweat. I snuggled toward Yairi's warm body and wondered what would happen if I really lost him. The thought didn't leave me until the morning light.

Chapter Four:
ITZHAK, SEPTEMBER 1939

TARNOBRZEG

When I was three years old, my older brother Shimon took me to the *cheder*, where I learned to read the letters of *sfat hakodesh*, the holy language. Shimon, who had already graduated from the *cheder*, was five years older than me. On the way there, he told me to be a good boy and not anger the rabbi, since he would beat my palm with a ruler if I did. Near the *cheder*, we stopped at a candy store. Mother had given us money to pay the rabbi for his lesson. The rabbi didn't like to be paid in coins, but Shimon, who had racked up harsh memories of the rabbi's ruler, had a plan.

I went into the *cheder* feeling ashamed and sat as close as I could to the rabbi, which was expected of his youngest student. I couldn't get Shimon's warnings out of my head about the rabbi's temper, especially while watching Shimon hand him the change he'd received at the candy store. The rabbi's expression eluded me, but Shimon looked pleased, so I let myself crack a small smile. On that day, and on the many days that followed, I was a good boy, didn't cause any trouble, wasn't rude, sat quietly in the corner of the classroom, and waited for the day to end, when Shimon would come pick me up and take me home. On those long days, I took refuge in the small chocolates the rabbi slipped into the palms of obedient pupils like me.

When Shimon arrived, I placed my small hand in his, took my hat, and out of the *cheder* we went. The streets bustled with passersby and peddlers selling their wares. There were voices of women carrying babies on their backs while encouraging their older children to keep up their pace. The laughter of children running through the narrow streets tickled my ears. When we passed the market, we stopped at the bakery stand where our cousin worked. She was happy to see us and placed two sweet, warm rolls into our hands. Shimon didn't let me out of his sight even for a second. He intended to keep his promise to Mother that he would get me home safely, today and every day. We left the bakery and jumped into a puddle; our faces stuffed with bread.

At home, Mother received us gently, with a warm smile and a loving embrace, and I could see in her eyes that she only needed my father to come home from work to feel entirely at ease. When he finally arrived, he patted our heads affectionately before turning to the table. After dinner, he sat with us and asked us about our day: What had we learned in *cheder*? Who had we played with? Who had we argued with? All the while, we were surrounded by aunts and uncles, most of whom hadn't married yet, so we were the object of admiration of the whole extended family.

Of all the days of the week, Shabbat was my favorite. Father woke up early and put on his handsomest suit. Mother woke up early, too, and thanks to her, we were fed and all set to go in our Shabbat clothes. We always went with Father to the synagogue, but not before Mother reminded us to be on our best behavior. My sisters stayed home, preparing the table for lunch, so that when we returned from shul, we would all eat together.

On the way to the synagogue, we were joined by others headed to the same place to pray. The synagogue was where the townspeople congregated; when we arrived, loud voices in song filled every corner of the room, extending out into the open air. Seated on one of the benches, I lifted my gaze to the ornate ceiling, where a painting of Jonah the prophet with a giant whale made the holiness of the Sabbath even more present. I remembered Father proudly placing a hand on each of our heads as we joined him in prayer, and after we had finished, he would leave them there tenderly, praying to God to watch over us.

At home, the Sabbath table welcomed us. The cholent lay proudly at the center, around which all our extended family members sat dressed in their Shabbat clothes. We, the younger children, wolfed down the food on our plates. Afterward, with Grandpa Eli's blessing, we rushed out to the yard where we started games that would continue until Shabbat was over the following evening.

The neighbor's children were also outside—Jews just like us who had also gulped down their Sabbath meal and come outside to play. Tzipke, the neighbor's daughter, was there with her brother, and so were Srul and Eliyahu, who were somewhere between my age and Shimon's, and my sisters, Shifra and Sima. We all played together. I loved Tzipke for being both beautiful and mischievous. She was a year younger than me, with eyes that were blue like the sea, or at least I thought until I saw the sea for the first time many years later. She had a rolling laugh, and when she began laughing, she was unstoppable, until eventually, we all found ourselves laughing with her. On the occasions when

Mother came outside and found Tzipke in stitches, she began to laugh as well, even without knowing the reason for Tzipke's laughter, and we'd all start laughing until we couldn't breathe anymore, and then we'd go back to playing.

I loved Tzipke, and she loved me, and although we were children, we vowed to get married when we grew up. We were sure that our parents would support us because they were such good friends themselves and always looked at us with a knowing smile. We didn't know that the world was about to turn on its head, or that God was laughing at us while we made our juvenile arrangements. On Saturday evening, after hours of play, we returned home for the *Havdala* service, and the fragrant smells from the spice box—the smells of being blessed and offering a blessing for the new week—have stayed with me ever since.

One morning, a loud explosion shook me from my sleep. I woke up frightened, and Mother called us to her and explained that the Germans were bombing Tarnobrzeg. A great commotion ensued. I remember people running from place to place, my mother's screams, and the fear that invaded every corner of the town. Following that day on which our town was so easily conquered, life did not return to normal. The Germans began marching in the streets as though built just for them. And they were even more cruel than before; many of us children thought of them as the devil incarnate. Soon the men started to be sent away—no one knew to where—among them my Uncle Pesach, may his memory be a blessing. He never returned home nor did any of the others who went with him. When community leaders asked the Germans where these men had gone, they responded with angry threats. "Don't you dare ask any questions, you dirty

Jews. You have no right."

"That is correct," our community leader replied to the Nazi. "We Jews have no rights, but we would like to know the whereabouts of the people who were sent away."

The Nazi held a gun to the heads of the community leader and his assistant, who took off his coat and said, "He'll do as he pleases." In front of hundreds of spectators who had gathered at the site, the Nazi shot our Jewish brethren in the head. They fell to the floor drenched in their own blood, and after that, nobody asked any more questions.

One Friday evening, as we gathered at the table for *kiddush*, someone began knocking loudly at the door. My father opened it, and three German soldiers barged in, demanding cigarettes. My father went to the closet and took out a few packs. The soldiers threw the cigarettes onto the floor and smashed them under the soles of their feet. Then they pulled the white tablecloth, with all the fancy silverware on it, and hurled it onto the floor. After they left, I burst into tears. Mother tried to calm me down, but I knew that she was just as afraid as I was.

***

A few days later, my ever-resourceful mother, after hearing that the Germans were coming, sent us all into hiding, while she stayed in the backyard, sweeping. When the Germans arrived, they asked my mother, "Where are the men of the house?" and she replied, "They're not here, they've been taken to work."

"And your husband—is he fighting against us?"

"No, no," my mother answered quickly, and kept on sweeping.

"If there are no men, you'll have to come with us," one of the Germans said. Setting the broom down, my mother left with the soldiers, who took her to an undisclosed location on the outskirts of the town, where she was assigned to hoisting heavy loads onto trucks. After an hour, she had already lost much of her strength and was terrified of what would happen if she became too exhausted to continue. Then, out of nowhere, an officer came toward her and asked, "What are you doing here, woman? I told them to bring only men!" The soldiers tried to explain that there weren't any men to bring, but the officer waved them away and barked, "Woman, go back to your home." Thus, my mother was saved—the first of many miracles that would occur during these war years.

Chapter Five: ICHU, OCTOBER 1939

POLAND

Mother woke us up in the morning and told me to quickly choose a toy that I wanted to keep, since only one toy was allowed. I turned my room upside down trying to decide. There was the ball that I had received from Aunt Pasia for my birthday, but Mother wouldn't hear of it, insisting, "It is too big, Ichu, I said one toy and not something big or heavy," while packing sets of clothing for each of us. I ended up taking a silver coin that Grandpa had given me for Hanukkah, making me swear that I would take care of it as if it were gold. I tucked it away safely, knowing we had been told not to take any money with us, and Mother had warned us as well—but who would discover a small, harmless coin? I told Mother that I didn't need any toys. I was almost seven years old, after all, and no longer a baby in need of playthings.

What Mother didn't know was that I had hidden the coin in a pocket of my coat. I prayed that nobody would find out, and I didn't say a word about it to anybody, not even to my brother Shimon. Mother told me to bring my prayer book. I went to get it and then to see what my older sisters were doing. They were helping Mother pack as fast as they could and asking, "What should we take? Warm clothing—it's the end of September, and it's already chilly." Shifra wanted to take the dress that Grandpa had sewn her for Rosh Hashana, but Mother wouldn't agree to it. They argued for a few minutes, and Shifra began to cry, while Mother scolded her quietly, explaining they should pack only logical, useful belongings, and that the moment they were allowed to return home, she could wear the elegant dress, white lace and all. In the midst of all this commotion, I saw Shimon pack his pocketknife, which he never left behind. "Those Nazis…I hate them," he mumbled. "Nobody will come near us, and if they do, they'll regret it," were the words of my valiant brother—no wonder I admired him so. When I was with him, nothing bad could happen to me.

Mother told Grandpa to hurry up and ran with Shifra to look for Father, saying that we'd all meet up in the center of the village. As she was leaving the house, I noticed that tears had welled up in her eyes. She kissed the mezuzah and was off, while we joined the stream of people pouring into the center of the village. When we were together again, Shifra and Mother gathered me and Shimon into their arms, while Grandpa placed his hand on Father's shoulder and kept it there.

Observing this family embrace, a short, scary-looking German shouted at us, while a Polish man translated: "Whoever is found in possession of money or jewelry will find themselves bleeding from their neck!" At this warning, Mother checked, and then rechecked, to make sure that none of us had brought along any valuables. Directing a stern gaze at the girls, she said, "This isn't a joke, you know." They both confirmed that they hadn't taken anything, whereas I said nothing, and clutched the coin inside my pocket. Suddenly, I heard shouting, followed by shots fired into the air. Mother held me close to her and covered my eyes, repeating over and over again that it was just noise. We began walking, without any idea where we were going or why we were leaving, and I almost started to cry. But Shimon caught my eye and made the funniest face I'd ever seen, so I smiled at him and held out my hand for him to take. When I had calmed down, I looked around for my good friend Tzipke, and saw her in the distance hiding in her mother's dress, but she didn't see me. More and more people arrived at the village entrance. At some point, Father went to ask something, and we lost sight of him, which worried Mother out of her mind, but Grandpa assured her that if she knew his son, she would know that he was sure to appear out of nowhere. And indeed, Father was waiting for us on the street corner, just like Grandpa had said.

When we were all together again, Grandpa suggested making for the forest, where they might come across a rabbit to cheer them up. Mother smiled at Grandpa, but I noticed that the wrinkle between her eyes was unusually deep. I didn't ask her why she was so worried since Father had told us to keep our voices at a whisper, at least until we got out of the village. He added that rabbits were afraid of noise, and Shimon winked at me, while Sima held back a smile trying to see if I'd bought his tale. I didn't care if it was true or not; there was enough noise around us that in any case we didn't stand a chance of finding a rabbit. I held Mother's hand so tightly that it was hard for her to wiggle her fingers.

Outside the village everything was much quieter. Only when we were deep inside the forest did I realize that we'd been walking for a long time, and that it had already become dark, and we couldn't see anything. From far away, we could hear the noise of plane engines and faraway gunshots coming closer. Father recited the *Shema Yisroel*, and I couldn't decide whether to join him or to hold Shimon's hand even tighter. I didn't want it to hurt, the way Mother's had. The walk seemed to never end, my legs were tired, and I was hungry and thirsty, but I didn't complain. I understood that this wasn't just any walk in the forest, but something much more. Eventually, Father said that we could stop to rest and plan how we would pass the night. We divided the two loaves of bread that Aunt Pasya had brought us. As we chewed in silence, Grandpa said that maybe we should walk a bit more, but Father said there was no point, we couldn't even see our own footsteps, so it would be better to go to sleep. We made beds of leaves to lie on, but the ground was too wet to start a fire, so we bunched up together to create heat, and after the evening prayer, I fell asleep immediately.

* * *

When I got up, everyone else was already awake. Mother had picked some berries, which had dried out on their bushes over the summer. Father led us through patches of trees, and when evening fell, we arrived at the shores of the Vistula River, where we met up with Tzipke's family. Tzipke's mother, Shayna, was trying to calm down baby Shloyme, but with every "shhhh," his cries only became stronger. Dozens of people stood on either side of the wide river, and in the midst of all the shouting, a Nazi suddenly loomed up before us. Before I could look away, I saw him grab Shloyme from his mother's arms and throw him into the cold, flowing current.

Shayna let out a shrill cry and fainted, and the Nazi pointed his gun at Tzipke's father, who managed to hold a steady gaze, his knees quivering. I began to cry, but Shimon said from the side of his mouth, "Stop, or they'll throw you into the water, too." I stopped and held his hand, while reaching for Mother's dress with my free hand. Meanwhile, Father had found a small raft hidden among the trees and was loading people onto it, two by two.

My father, the hero, how proud I was of him, always finding simple solutions to complicated problems. When we arrived on the other side of the river, we were told by the Russians to wait. When I asked Father why and for how long, he replied that there was plenty of time, and no need to rush. A rainstorm ensued, causing us to huddle together to keep warm, and Father found a branch that sheltered our heads, at least for the most part.

* * *

We sat in that spot for a week or so. Once a day, we were given a bit of dry bread and potatoes and told to keep waiting, and that eventually *they'd* be told what to do with us. Finally, after what seemed like forever, a few of the Russians came over and instructed us to get on a train to Lvov, so we did. It was nice because I got to sit down, and I was no longer wet or freezing. The feeling didn't last for long; when we arrived, we had to find someplace to sleep for the night. I was too hungry and tired to care where.

Lvov was a ruin of rubble thanks to all the buildings the Nazis had destroyed. We went into one of these buildings, and Mother began to arrange it as if it were our home. Soon we were joined by legions of lice, and we couldn't stop scratching.

I almost forgot—after two days in our new "home," more families appeared on our street. I was happy to discover Tzipke's family among them. The expression on her face when she saw me was worth everything, and from that moment on, we were inseparable. Her mother looked so sad, and Tzipke told me that she hadn't stopped crying even for a second. I told her I was sure her baby brother was in heaven now, and Tzipke said that I was right because he was the cutest baby she'd ever met. And then we were silent.

There was a street next to a bakery where they baked fresh bread. I asked if she wanted to go there with me to smell it, since the smell made me feel at home, and I had barely eaten anything in weeks. Tzipke said it sounded like a great idea and that she also missed the smell of bread, like the scent that used to waft through our village. I gave Tzipke my hand, and she held it tightly. I smiled at her, hoping she couldn't see how hot my face had become, and when I saw Shifra and Sima coming toward us, I let go, and we ran to them.

From that day, on every day besides Saturday, we strolled wherever we wanted, whenever we wanted, and became better friends than ever. Tzipke's mother behaved so strangely, never asking Tzipke where she was going or when she would be back. She didn't do anything besides stare at the wall all day long. When I mentioned this to my mother, she stopped me short and explained that Shayna was going through a difficult time, and we all needed to be kind to her because of what had happened to baby Shloyme, so I tried to be on my best behavior.

One evening, a few Russians arrived wearing unfamiliar uniforms and demanded that all the families living in our building report to the train station early the next morning. They refused to answer any of our questions and told the Zak family, who had come with us from the village and lived in the same burned-out building as we did, to come with them at once.

Nobody uttered a sound. My mother motioned to us to keep our mouths shut. The Zak family quickly gathered their few belongings. They turned to us, and the father said he would pray for everyone, and hoped that we would pray for them, too, and then they left. I didn't get a chance to say goodbye to his children because I thought they would be back soon enough, but they never came back. I never saw them again. I didn't understand why Father and Mother had told us to gather our things, or why they told us to be prepared to move quickly in the morning, but at the crack of dawn, two men came out to count us: Our family and grandparents, two of our aunts, and Tzipke's family, along with two other families who we'd met in Lvov. Father told us to remain quiet and not answer any questions that might be directed to us. Only he would do the talking. My father knew a few words in Russian, so when someone said something to him, he nodded and said something back. I didn't understand a thing, but soon it became clear that we needed to leave immediately, and Father instructed us not to leave anything behind. Once outside the destroyed building, we followed two unfamiliar men in silence until we arrived at a truck, onto which we were all loaded and driven to the train station. Then we were all loaded onto the train, leaving Lvov for an unknown destination. Fingering the coin in my pocket, I decided that no matter what happened, wherever I ended up, I'd still be the richest boy in the world.

CHAPTER SIX: ITZHAK, OCTOBER 1939

POLAND

There are days one doesn't forget, no matter how much time has passed. We had heard rumors about the deportation but refused to believe them.

Father woke up at the crack of dawn to head out for the nearby village where he had found a few days' work. Soon after he left, the order was issued: All the Jews were to be rounded up in the central square. We were told to take money, jewelry, and some clothing, and to arrive no later than ten in the morning. Tardiness could amount to death.

When Mother said that we were "leaving the village," I didn't exactly understand what she meant. For a short while? For a trip? Where were we going? I don't think she knew that our lives would never return to the way they'd been before, that familiar faces would disappear from our lives, that some of our beloved family members wouldn't survive the difficult war. Mother said not to take anything with us, only a coat and a hat. That was all. Before we left, I went over to my hiding spot underneath the floor of my room and removed the lucky coin I'd gotten for Hannukah from my grandparents. I didn't say a word to anyone about it because I knew I wouldn't be allowed to take it with me. I grasped it tightly and held out my arm to Grandma. She looked at me and said that everything would be okay and told me not to worry. She even patted my head. We stood at the doorstep clutching each other, and amidst the storm of people shouting and praying, we found ourselves streaming toward the center of the village.

Suddenly, Mother thought of Father and became anxious by the possibility of him being late, and she told Shifra that she would be the best alibi if they went out to look for him since her blonde hair made her look like a local Polish girl. They found him, which was a relief for all the aunts and cousins who had left without him and had been worried about his whereabouts. The Germans had given specific instructions: Jewelry and clothing were to be passed along to them and whoever didn't comply would be shot. They conducted a search, not sparing the small children, even my sister Sima. A soldier came up to her and wrenched open the buttons of her coat. Children who were found with jewelry were taken off to the side with their family, and we never heard what their fate was. Among these families, there was one girl named Rivkale, who was my sister Sima's friend. Many years afterward, Sima would wake up crying at night from "bad dreams," in which Rivkale, her brother, and her sister were in a dark place, shaking with tears.

Vehicles rumbled into the center of town, with German soldiers peering out of each window. A Polish official stood by and translated what they barked: A few people had already been shot, so being smart alecks wouldn't help us, and we shouldn't dare try to sneak anything behind their backs—money, jewelry, or otherwise. We were to exit the town and go to Yavoriv, which was over a hundred and sixty kilometers away, and to where all the Jews had been sent from the surrounding villages. The area had become part of Russia as a result of the Molotov-Ribbentrop Pact, which divided Poland into two parts, one Russian and one German. The pact was made for a duration of ten years, but the Germans exploited it by expanding further into Europe.

Tzipke and her family were also in Yavoriv and seemed shocked to be there, like everybody else. Her mother was crying inconsolably, while her father tried in vain to comfort her. While holding her mother's hand, Tzipke searched for my eyes then gave me a look so helpless and distraught, I'll never be able to forget it. I hoped that the cursed Nazis wouldn't search her for jewelry; even if her mother had any, it was probably not worth very much. Tzipke came from a family even poorer than mine. To my relief, the Nazi who was inspecting the rows of families passed by her, and I felt her breathing ease, even from a distance. Afterward, in the midst of the chaos, I looked away for a minute, and when I looked back, she was gone.

We all began walking toward the outskirts of the village. I saw Father whisper something to Mother, and then he turned to us and said there was no reason to walk on the main road, and we should take a different route since eventually we'd get to the same place. I searched for some solace in my mother's unreadable expression but found none, and then saw my classmate Yasha who used to sit next to me in *cheder*. Yasha was quiet and studious. I would play with him during recess, and when the rabbi walked among the desks, Yasha would quietly give me some candy that he'd snuck into class. I wanted to run over to Yasha and tell him to come with us, but he simply stared at me, while Mother held onto my hand tightly, restricting my movement. It was the last time I saw him. Giving in to Mother's grip, I went along quietly after her and Father. We walked in total silence, listening in horror as the noisy planes bombed the main road that many of our fellow townspeople had taken—the same road which we had avoided.

The walk was long and cumbersome, especially for the children and the elderly. Father, who saw a Polish man he recognized with his carriage, asked him to help us, or at least the children. He initially refused but then softened and agreed, so the children and grandparents were lifted onto the carriage for a kilometer or two, until he stopped and asked us to walk again. From the moment night fell, screams were heard from every point in space—commands and cries for help. When it was completely dark, the screams sounded even scarier. We didn't know if it was the Poles who were shouting, or the Germans descending on people and robbing them. We kept on walking—freezing, thirsty, and hungry—all night long, hardly stopping to rest, and in the morning, we continued until we arrived at the wide river.

On the riverbank, we were once again surrounded by threatening Germans. Scores of people were milling about in total confusion. The Poles had supplied small boats to ferry passengers from the Polish to the Russian side. The Vistula marked Poland's border. Its eastern side was part of the USSR and the western side belonged to Germany. Poland lost its identity until the end of the war. When we returned, it was only to discover our former lives in ruin, and nothing there belonged to us anymore. The Poles, with their icy hearts and hatred of Jews pumping through their veins, didn't hesitate to tell Jews returning from the war to get back onto the trains and continue traipsing the continent. But that is another story entirely.

We stood for hours by the river, waiting for our turn to cross. I recognized one woman from our village who had been unable to get pregnant for years until a miracle happened, and she gave birth to a baby boy. She was put on a rickety boat with her husband and son, and the boat quickly began to fill with water. She cried for help, but the Germans called out to let them drown. Luckily, a Polish man helping with the boats saw her S.O.S. and didn't understand what the Germans were saying, so he rowed to them and brought them safely to the other side. Thus, they evaded death.

As the hours ticked by, we saw some boats arrive safely on the other side, along with many that didn't make it, the fate of their passengers sealed. Father, seeing our distress, said that fear was useless, and we ought to exercise caution instead. He told us that when he was a young boy, some anti-Semitic Polish boys once tried to provoke him into a violent confrontation. His attempts to stop them failed, and they beat him to the ground, but he stood up and fought back even more impressively, and from that day, they didn't bother him anymore.

Father said we needed to demonstrate resilience because "Even when we're afraid, we shouldn't show weakness, for that is how you survive." Mother decided to take action. She identified an older-looking German officer with a kind face and brought me over to him. I remember that I kept crying about my exhaustion and hunger. In her broken German, Mother asked the officer if he could help us cross the river. She explained that her children were tired and hungry, and if he would be so kind as to help us, he would be blessed in return. Telling us to wait, the officer gestured to a Polish man just returning from the other side of the river with a sturdy-looking boat. Mother immediately called us over. The moment the boat arrived, she whispered to Father that he should go first then ushered everybody else inside until the boat was packed, and she had no room to get on herself. Father began to say something, but before the words could come out of his mouth, the Polish man had kicked the boat from the shore and sent it sailing toward the Russian side with Mother left behind. We didn't say a word, but only prayed we'd make it to the other side, and Mother would, too. When we arrived, Father exclaimed, "I can't believe that I left her on the other side and still made it out alive," and we all began to cry. But Father said that Mother was strong and smart and that he had no doubt she would join us very soon. We believed him and sat down to wait. And indeed, a few hours later, when it had already become dark, we saw her approaching in one of the boats. If Mother hadn't urged Father onto the boat, there's no way to know if Father would have survived alone. We were united once again. We had arrived in Russia and could only hope for the best. Father relaxed and whispered something to Mother, whose eyes were filled with tears. On the Russian side of the river, there was an interim camp populated by hundreds of thousands of people. The Russians had no idea what to do with all of us. At first, there were mostly drunk soldiers, dancing and drinking. They gave us candy, which made us hopeful that we would eventually blend in as Jews, and perhaps our lives could return to normal. Once evening arrived, it started to rain, and we had no shelter, so we all huddled together to keep warm until morning came. In the morning, we were informed that we were being transferred to Lvov, which had originally been a Polish city but had become Russian after the pact between the Germans and the Russians. My parents thought that we would finally have a decent living situation, but when we arrived, we found the city under piles of rubble—it had been bombed. Although most of the structures had roofs for a change, the conditions were harsh, with no infrastructure to speak of. We lived a few families to one room, each family picking their own corner, and the lice were relentless.

In Lvov, we were considered displaced people deprived of any basic rights. Adults were prohibited from working, but my father collected all kinds of trinkets and tried to sell them at the market. One time, an angry man approached us, flipped over the box on which the trinkets lay, and expelled my father from the market, his expression dripping with disdain. The living conditions in Lvov were difficult: The winter was unbearable—extremely cold, with very little to eat—the Russians provided a bit of dry bread, that was all—and barely any room to move. Without beds, we had to sleep directly on the freezing floor. That is how we lived for a few months, until one day, out of nowhere, Aunt Mira, my father's sister, arrived from Krakow carrying a small suitcase with her. Brave Mira, who was married and a mother of a baby less than two years old, had decided to cross the battle lines to see us. How happy we were, us children, and how much fear there was in the faces of her parents, my grandparents, when she appeared in Lvov. She told us that she had missed us too terribly, so she had decided to come on her own because if her sister, Brunia, had joined her, it would have been much more difficult to hide. In the small suitcase, she carried children's clothing, which my parents could trade for a bit of food. When

Aunt Brunia came to visit us in Tarnobrzeg, she would measure us first with her eyes, and then with a yardstick to see how much we'd grown. She'd play with us and laugh with us, our beloved aunt, and we were all disappointed that she hadn't come to see us in Lvov. I don't remember how Mira got home, but she somehow made it back safely.

One day, after a few months in Lvov, Russian government representatives arrived to ask if we wanted to return to our homes. Naturally, there was a consensus among our townspeople: Yes, we'd like to return to Poland. My sister Sima told me later that she was angry everybody's response had been the same. Why would they want to return to Poland when the Poles had come after us, right alongside their Nazi friends? They had probably answered that way because it was the most human response—the prospect of going home was so appealing compared to the existing situation that they were able to set aside all they had endured. The response of the townspeople, among them my parents, saved our lives. One night, Russian soldiers entered our rooms and sent us to the Russian steppe, claiming that we were disloyal to the Russian regime, and therefore, traitors. Only one family, who was not from our village and had not requested to go home, was left behind. Later on, the Germans conquered Lvov and sent its Jewish residents to the death camps. Our lives had been saved once again.

CHAPTER SEVEN: MAYA, 2018

TEL AVIV

When I got to the part where young Ichu recounts the Nazis tossing the baby into the water, I was so horrified that I had to stop writing for the day. I thought about Ichu's mother and father, wandering about without any food or shelter—the basic facets of life that we take for granted. It was difficult for me to understand how someone could throw a child into a river to his death, and how a young boy witnessing such an act would have to go through life with such a terrorizing memory etched into his brain. I closed my computer, put on the headphones Yair had bought me for my birthday, and hoped that the loud music would allay my thoughts. I left the house, slamming the front door behind me, and entered an entire world waiting outside that had evaded me for the past few days. The sun was shining but not too hot, and the morning breeze refreshed me. The bustling streets grounded me, making me feel sane again, which was something I desperately needed. I thought about the story I was writing about the life of a man who I didn't entirely know, yet felt so close to, who bore the scars of so many difficult years. He had survived the war, that cursed war, lived his whole life in the shadow of a different life that could have been. Above all, I wondered about his heart, his wounded heart: Had it ever stood a chance of survival?

The music overtook my thoughts, and I set out with purpose to the neighborhood park. I would walk around it a few times and head back home. When I arrived, there were two elderly people sitting on a worn-out bench. They looked at me and smiled, acknowledging me with a nod. I nodded back and said, "Hello, it's such a beautiful day today, not too hot," and they responded in a heavy foreign accent, "Hello there, good day to you." I began walking again but was now plagued by another thought: Were they too survivors? What ordeals might they have gone through? Where were they from? What had they borne witness to?

I tried to enjoy the moment: The atmosphere of the park, the birds chirping merrily, telling tales of their tumultuous lives—lives that I would never understand. I smiled and headed back home. In the living room, I fell onto the couch and drank water straight out of the bottle that I'd brought with me from my empty fridge.

* * *

In the neighborhood supermarket, employees were stocking the fruit and vegetable shelves. After both Abed and Yossi pointed out the killer price of the organic strawberries that had arrived in the morning, I took three cartons instead of one. Worst case, I could always make a fruit salad. I continued down the other aisles, filling my cart to capacity, with the plan to properly arrange the fridge before picking up the kids from school. When I got home, I discovered the fridge full beyond capacity. I looked at the bulging appliance helplessly, not knowing whether to laugh or cry or what to do with the items piled on the kitchen table, not to mention the pots of food I had made that morning. "Time for a new fridge," I thought. As if.

In the evening, when Yair came home and opened the fridge, an avalanche of strawberries tumbled out. His face turned pink, and I didn't know if it was from surprise, or from the strawberry juice that had splattered onto his head. The children stopped what they were doing and didn't know how to react. They looked at Yairi's face, and then at mine, and when I burst out laughing, they did, too. When Yairi saw us all laughing, he took a huge strawberry and stuffed it in his mouth. Avishay said, "*Aba*, I think this is the funniest day of my life." Rushing over to help him pick up the mess from the floor, I apologized for my impulsive behavior at the store. Yairi looked at me and said, "What's going on here? There isn't a centimeter of space in the fridge."

After he went to the bedroom to change his clothes, I asked the children to wash their hands, and I carried the youngest over to the sink to help her. Then I served dinner: A plain omelet for Dana, scrambled eggs for Avishay, and small pieces of omelet for little Gali, who was waiting impatiently for her turn. "I want a strawberry, I want a strawberry!" she demanded, so I cut up a few and called out, "Who else wants a strawberry? Who will be the lion who likes strawberries today?" The children all raised their hands, and I prepared some strawberries for them, too, then an omelet with vegetables for Yairi, along with two pieces of toast, and finally, I made a sunny side up egg for myself and sat down to eat. Freshly dressed, Yairi returned and sat down in front of his plate. "Just don't offer me any strawberries; I've had enough for a year," he said. I smiled at him, and slowly the winds calmed as we filled our stomachs.

One by one, we asked the children how their days had been. What was the best thing that had happened to them? Little Gali finished the food on her plate and asked for more vegetables. I was proud of my little girl for liking fruit and vegetables so much. While she tackled another tomato, Avishay told us about his snack break, which had been going fine until his friend Ron asked to trade his sandwich with chocolate spread. I thought to myself that no matter what had happened at school today or tomorrow or next year, my children would never lack for bread, and a mixture of grief and relief clouded my head. Dana told me about her new gym teacher, who had come to substitute for the pretty teacher who was out sick. "She's a lot of fun," Dana said, adding that today in class they had learned the rules of dodgeball and even started to play, but before she knew it class was over, and she hoped that next time they would "start playing immediately, without too much talk."

Avishay was surprised to hear about the new teacher and said that he hoped this teacher would let the boys play soccer, since "Soccer is a boy's sport and not for girls." Dana and I looked at him, and Dana said that soccer was for everyone, not just for boys. Trying to avoid an argument, I told them that when I was young, I had loved playing dodgeball, and even played on the school team. Dana said she felt just like me, that the game seemed "really cool," and Avishay didn't say anything, so we kept eating quietly. I noticed the slang the children were acquiring from year to year, and at a pace with which my generation couldn't keep up. I also thought about how nice Yairi had been during dinner. Maybe his workload was lightening, and that with less stress to deal with, my Yairi would finally come back to us, and we could be a normal family again. I really hoped so.

Chapter Eight:
ITZHAK, NOVEMBER 1939,
ON THE WAY TO LABOR CAMP

From that day on, we became prisoners of the communist regime, and we were expelled from "sensitive areas"—that is, areas that sat on the borders and were susceptible to German intrusion. It was decided that residents such as us, whose loyalties were held suspect, steer clear of those areas, which turned out to work in our favor. At every stage of the war, when it was deemed that the front lines were getting too close, the Russians would pluck us from wherever we were and deposit us deeper inside the mainland, driving us away from the most intense fighting zones, even if their intention wasn't to save our lives.

One night, we heard echoes of cannons, and in the middle of the night, we were woken up and told to gather our few belongings. From one of the less crowded streets in Lvov, we were loaded onto a truck and taken to the train station. At the crack of dawn, at the train station on the outskirts of the city, soldiers went from family to family, asking a series of questions that would determine who would be sent to a labor camp and who to a different type of camp. Our extended family was separated. My uncle Noah, a single man, was sent to a labor camp, as were my uncles Naphtali and Dov together with my father's parents. We didn't find out what happened to them until long after the war—Naphtali had died from a snake bite, and his parents, who were heartbroken, died shortly afterward. Tzipke's family, standing close to ours, received an identical sentence and were loaded onto the same train car as us. The Russians had decided they would come to the labor camp with us. That's all we knew—labor camp—that was all. We didn't know where, and we didn't know how long it would take to arrive at this camp that had been chosen for us. We didn't know much of anything. Honestly, I didn't really care where we were going. All I cared about was that Tzipke's family and mine would continue together.

We got on the train, where dozens of people were crammed into a cattle car. The door locked behind us and darkness descended. Slowly, our eyes became accustomed to the dark. I remember looking around me, making sure that my family was still there, that nobody had been left behind by mistake. The train rumbled onward for long days, perhaps even weeks, and when it stopped, we were forbidden from getting off. During the day, the children were all bunched up onto one side and left to their own devices. There's one game we played that I still remember. We would pass a small object, such as an article of clothing, from hand to hand, and whoever received the object had to guess what it was. Hours of such games helped us pass the time to an unknown destination. We received food twice a day—in the morning, some kind of sticky oatmeal, and in the evening, a bit of moldy bread.

At one point, a guard allowed me to get off the train for a few minutes. I felt like the king of the world just from my feet touching the ground long enough for me to stretch my bones. Grandpa filled many of our hours with stories. All the children gathered around him as he told us about the first World War, how he had barely managed to escape death and had been enlisted into the Polish army. We laughed at his descriptions of bureaucratic officials whom he had managed to convince that he was unfit for war. After a few weeks, the train came to a halt, and we were instructed to report to the coal room for a shower. We were all itchy from lice, and the scratching made our skin blotchy. First the men, and then the women, undressed and passed their clothing to the guard. We were given soap, and above us, a showerhead streamed ice-cold water. With our sanitized clothing, we returned to the cattle car. After a few days, the lice returned to their usual lodgings. Then, just as I was beginning to think this ordeal would never end, the train stopped abruptly, and to our astonishment, we were ordered off it with our meager belongings.

At first, I didn't entirely understand what the problem was, but Father explained—we hadn't arrived at a station. So where were we? Outside, it was snowing and bitterly cold. With our belongings, we got off the train where horse-drawn trolleys were expecting us. We walked for a while, probably about a thousand people in all, with the horses lugging the trolleys holding our things, until we arrived at our destination: A thick forest, devoid of any man-made structures—no cabins, no infrastructure, nothing. An outcry ensued at the sight of the forest, with people shouting, "Where have you brought us? Where will we live?" to which the soldiers merely responded, "These were our orders, the camps are full, we couldn't continue." We all looked at each other helplessly, and Father said, "Let's figure out how we can prepare for nightfall. Tomorrow is a new day." Kochak, a government representative, stuck a plank of wood into the ground and wrote the number 19 on top. The name of our new camp—19. That was all, 19, in the middle of nowhere.

Chapter Nine:
ICHU, NOVEMBER 1939

ON THE WAY TO LABOR CAMP

When the train door was flung open, I couldn't see anything, but Mother pushed me inside, and Shifra told me to sit quietly and wait. I looked for Tzipke and her family, but it was too dark to make out anything more than silhouettes. Soon I began to cry and suddenly heard Tzipke calling, "Ichu, why are you crying? We're all here, everything's okay." We were shoved, scores of people, into the tiny car which smelled of cow manure. I said to Shimon that soon we'd all be mooing, and Mother scolded my impure speech. Gradually, we got used to the dark, and I saw that the cattle car was not so much a cattle car as it was a sardine tin, the kind that Father sometimes brought from the market. There were people without anything to lean on, but we had lucked out and snagged a corner. Mother asked me to move over to make room for an elderly woman, who I identified as our neighbor, Chanuchka's grandma. She looked older than I remembered her, which was saying a lot, since she had always looked at least one hundred years old, and now she looked almost one hundred and twenty, or at the very least one hundred and nineteen. A quick thought entered my head that she didn't have very long left to live, and how lucky I was for having Grandpa Eliyahu, who wasn't as old. I looked at him and loved him even more than usual. When the train started moving, Mother told me that I could lean on her, so I did, for many hours. I didn't notice that I had fallen asleep, and when I woke up, I saw that someone had thrown stinky, dry bread into the train car, and everybody was pouncing on it. In our village, my father had been respected as a man of integrity, resourcefulness, and action. He took the dry bread and the car fell silent. He then began dividing it among the families equally, but after gobbling it down, we were still hungry. I was afraid to say something to Mother because Shimon might laugh at me, so instead I said, "This bread will keep me going for at least two days."

Shimon looked at me and burst out laughing. He said, "In the best case, that bread will keep me going for another ten minutes," and I began to laugh, too.

Then Shifra joined in with Sima, and Tzipke looked at me as if I were a hero and let out a hearty chuckle, and I thought to myself that she had the best laugh I'd ever heard. I was so happy that she and her family were traveling with us in the same crowded car because that way at least we could play and wouldn't be bored. Suddenly, a wave of laughter had overtaken our train car, and nobody understood what was happening; I thought that perhaps laughter was preferable to tears since I suspected I was far from being the only one who had been left hungry.

When everybody settled down, the train car became quiet again, and the wheels finally began to turn. Two small children who had been crying for ages eventually fell asleep, and an eerie silence took over for the next hours, or maybe days, as long as the train kept rumbling. I thought it would never stop, but every time I asked when we were going to get there, I was hushed and told we'd get there when we got there. At some point, I don't even remember when I stopped asking.

One day, the train came to a halt, and someone from outside shouted at us to move toward the first compartment for a shower. I was thrilled since I couldn't stop itching, and everything hurt. The women were separated from the men, and while I waited my turn, we were told to hand over our clothing, and I saw how thin Father and Shimon had become. Then I saw myself and thought I looked exactly how I felt: like a hungry child. I almost started laughing but stopped myself. The sight of everybody jumping around under a freezing stream of water was especially funny. Afterward, we were given back our clothes, which were warm but still very dirty. I didn't care—I got dressed and followed Father and Shimon back to our compartment, where we found all the women, as clean as could be, which wasn't very. Everyone exchanged insecure glances, and then Father said to Mother, "Chayuchka, I've never seen you look more beautiful." That's what he said to her, in front of everyone, and I agreed with him, since my mother is truly the most beautiful in the world, not only now, but always. Mother laughed and told him that he was exaggerating as usual. Tzipke's father started to say something to Tzipke's mother, but she wouldn't have any part of it. As usual, she was staring into a corner, with the same expression she had worn since the baby drowned, the same inability to laugh or smile. Swallowing his words, Tzipke's father reached over to hug his wife, and the train began rumbling once again.

Chapter Ten:
MAYA, 2018

TEL AVIV

Every morning, I woke up early, took the kids to school, cleaned, cooked, ran the washing machine and folded its contents, booked doctor's appointments, and consulted appointments for Avishay's ADHD. I wondered if I should be worrying about Dana, too, for whom homework was a nightmare, despite her being such a good, quiet girl. It drained us both of our energies, and I was reminded of a judgmental neighbor who had once asked me, "If you don't work, what do you do all day?"

Gali was sick and stayed home for a few days, and I could only dream of writing at the computer, where I had left little Ichu somewhere in between Poland and Russia. Driving between errands, I listened to classical music and wove plots together, but when I tried to put them into prose, they escaped me. Only a week later did I find myself sitting quietly in front of the computer, staring at it. It stared back at me, and we settled into each another's silence. "A room of my own," I thought to myself, like the one Virginia Woolf had written about, a shut-off space, quiet, which nobody could enter or exit but me. That's all she had asked for herself. Maybe, when the kids were a bit older, we would be able to convert the playroom into a study, and this time it would be mine, since Yair didn't work from home anyway and didn't really need a study. I would give anything to begin the novel I'd been dreaming of writing.

I almost got up to do the laundry, but something lured me deeper into my chair— my characters, who awaited me from a cold, alienated world, and for whom the least I could do was not leave them there. I thumbed through the pages backward, trying to reconnect, and eventually sunk deep into the story. I didn't stop writing until the phone startled me.

It was my mother, calling to ask if we would be able to host Shavuot dinner this year. I said I'd let her know and hung up, but my train of thought had been broken, and I couldn't get back into the story. Saving the document, I got up and went into the kitchen to make coffee, before remembering that I had missed my hair appointment that I'd booked more than two weeks ago. I called and begged them to take me, but my appointment had already been snatched up by someone else. My white hairs would have to remain white for another few days. Slapping a hat on my head, I went out to pick up the kids from school.

Chapter Eleven:
ITZHAK, FEBRUARY 1940

CAMP 19, RUSSIA

When we were unloaded from the trains, the guard who had accompanied our journey also got off. His name was Kozak. He was Russian, with a wide frame and a deep voice. Driving a numbered plank into the ground, he declared that this would be our plot: 19. He also said that those who were strong and resourceful would survive, and everybody else would perish. Of course, he was right—out of the one thousand people who had come with us, only five hundred remained after two years. Many died from disease, from the cold, or from the overall neglect and unhygienic conditions in which we lived.

We arrived at the steppe in February, when Russia's frosty cold was especially unforgiving. There were few hours of daylight. It became light late and dark early, and from the moment the sun set, we tried to stick together, close to the fire that burned around the clock. We were in a forest that had nothing in it besides trees and many hungry, empty stomachs. When Mother murmured a prayer, my sisters began to cry, but she stopped them immediately and told them to prepare for nightfall, and to save their tears for when they really needed them. Mother motioned me to her, hugged me close and explained that these were our circumstances, and we had to learn to live with them. Reminding me that as long as we were together, everything would be okay, she sent me over to join the men preparing makeshift bedding on the ground.

In the forest, there were a few small, stuffy cabins, definitely not sufficient for the number of people who had come to Camp 19. When we understood that they were also full of fleas and lice, Father, Shimon, the uncles, and I collected some branches and started a fire to warn them—and the other horrible forest beasts—away. Huddled up together, we prayed there would come a day when we'd be able to go home. It didn't cross our minds that the long years of scarcity had just begun. That first night was especially long. We slept outside, listening to the sounds of the night, to the shrieks of the animals, praying they wouldn't come near. Father said not to worry, he was watching over us, and we should try to fall asleep. At those words, my head immediately rolled to the side, and I learned only the next day that some bad animals had approached us, and the men had driven them away with wood planks and fire. The next day, Kozak explained which trees were best for building our cabins, and we got to work. Shimon and I helped by carrying the largest branches we could find. Kozak told us how to extract the right amount of tree sap to attach the branches to one another and how to insulate the cabin from the cold. We went from tree to tree, looking for just the right one, and after we cut it down, we chopped it up with a saw someone had given us. Then we moved on to the next tree, and that's how the trees were collected for the construction of the two cabins—one for us and the other for our relatives. Grandpa would stay in ours.

Then I saw them. They looked like cavemen, neglected, wild,

and frightening. Kozak told us they were the locals, the Mari people, who didn't see themselves as part of Soviet Russia, but that for the time being nobody cared enough to bother them about it. I wasn't sure if he was speaking about them condescendingly or with admiration, but there was apprehension in his eyes. Father, who wasn't afraid of anybody in the world, walked over to them with a big warm smile, and for a moment, it appeared to be the start of an unlikely friendship: Father, a slight-framed Jew, wearing black, dirty all over, not having seen a proper shower in weeks, meeting these massive people clad in various leathers, their hair running free, mumbling in an unfamiliar language. Even though he didn't understand a word of what they were saying, Father gestured his hand toward them as a sign of peace, and they smiled and laughed heartily, exposing their toothless mouths. They pointed at us, then at themselves, and afterward at the huge bear that they had hunted straight from his cave, as if to ask why we were building these huts and how we were planning to survive the harsh winter in this never-ending forest.

Slowly but surely, the cabin construction project took off, and we all rallied for its completion, including my beloved grandpa. The camp's chaos eventually gave way to a daily schedule, with its most reliable constant being the fire that warmed us day and night. Kozak made sure that everybody received a small daily serving of sorghum grain with a bit of salt and sugar, but most of the time we were still hungry. Grandpa Eli had an original idea: He would add a ton of salt to his bread, and by doing so, be thirsty instead of hungry. When we finished building the cabin, Kozak called us to come with him. He had gotten ahold of some stoves, and with the help of oxen, we brought them to the cabins.

Finally, we could warm ourselves inside, as well as heat up our meager meals. But even with this slight heat, and a roof above our heads to protect us against the wind, rain, and cold, we were so weak and thin that often all we wanted to do was simply make it to the next day.

The winter was particularly long and harsh. There were long days of frost, our clothing began to tatter, food was scarce, and people became sick and died because of a lack of medical supplies. Despite all this, we got out of bed every day, chopped trees, ate whatever was available, and when there was nothing to forage, we feigned satisfaction from our daily sorghum meal and remained hungry. The local Maris, who had survived many generations in this thick forest, taught us the secret of spirit and determination. From them, we learned how to keep our bodies warm, and with the melting of the snows and the long-awaited arrival of summer, how to forage mushrooms safely and which berries were edible. We were in awe of these people for appearing so invincible.

The passing months brought with them the spring. Leaves began to peek out from between the trees, and the soil slowly exposed itself. Mother and Father reminded us that we still had the most cherished thing in the world: one another. They would always take care of us, and we knew that whatever happened, we were protected. At the end of winter, the Russians had suddenly remembered to send us some fabrics, and my grandpa had his hands full, sewing comfortable clothing for women and men alike, with the help of my mother, sisters, and young aunts. I couldn't have been happier to receive my new pants. Finally, pants that actually wrapped around my waist! When Grandpa handed them to me, I immediately went to hop around in the forest, careful not to damage the fabric. It was pure joy. I promised to take care of them just as I'd taken care of my Sabbath clothes at home, clothes which appeared in my memories every night. I missed my warm bed, but when I slept on the stacked branches next to Shimon, I made sure not to show him even one tear, so that he wouldn't laugh at my "weakness."

When summer came, we dipped into the nearby river, from which we also pumped water. It now flowed freely, unlike during the winter when we'd shaved off slivers of ice from the river's surface to melt in the stove. Our family, like the other exiles, continued to practice our Judaism devoutly. We counted the days by the moon to keep track of the holidays, and still knew the regular prayers by heart. When the Sabbath greeted us every week, we cleaned ourselves up as much as possible, and whatever food there was, we imagined as a feast. Mother lit a branch in lieu of Sabbath candles, and we were thankful for the bit of bread that we had, over which Grandpa said a blessing. After we ate, Father took the time to say a few words on the weekly Torah portion, and we all felt the joy of the Sabbath in its fullness.

Chapter Twelve: MAYA, 2018

TEL AVIV

For weeks, every day of writing was a full-blown war with myself. On the one hand, Itzhak's story was waiting to be written, but my life didn't always lend itself to smooth, uninhibited progress, and my conscience was pained by the image of the slight, elderly Itzhak waiting patiently for the day when he could finally share his story with the world. One morning, I finally sat down to work and then the deluge: What was new on Facebook? What was going on in Israel and in the world? Which emails were still awaiting my reply? My thoughts were disconnected from my actions; frenetically, I moved from one tab to another, before finally putting on some relaxing music and finishing my rounds peeking into the online lives of other people. Once again, I sank into the story, imagining places I'd never visited, characters whose lives were marred by that never-ending war in which so many family members and friends were lost, leaving those who remained changed forever. Every person has his own journey, each one challenging in its own right, but the journey undergone by Itzhak's family taught me every day anew the meaning of fortitude and perseverance, and of the human need to care for our loved ones and those around us. And to live, simply to live.

Over the past few days, Yairi has cut himself off again, and

I'm struggling to crack his hard shell. We barely speak, only saying things like, "Don't forget to buy bread and tomatoes," or "Don't forget to pay the gardener." I tried to check up on him a few times and ask how things were going. He claimed that everything was fine, that work had just been piling up, but there was nothing to worry about. I did my best not to burden him with house chores and kept my questions to a minimum. He began coming home late, always with a somber expression, and I minimized my presence so as not to rattle him further, hoping the smile would eventually return on its own. But it didn't seem to help. I noticed that the children were shying away from him as well, trying to avoid his unexpected outbursts but that didn't stop them from jumping into his arms the moment he walked in the door. In those moments, I stood back to observe the man with whom I shared my life and asked myself what was going on inside his head. I had no way of knowing if he didn't tell me, and it was clear that work was not his only burden. Yairi no longer seemed happy to see me; he no longer wrapped his arms around me or kissed me as he had done for so many years. Instead, he made a beeline for the kitchen, grabbed something to eat, and disappeared behind his desk. I desperately missed our family dinners, but soon I stopped waiting for him, instead making sure that by the time he came home, the children had already eaten and showered.

* * *

The morning started out with an argument. Yairi was in a rush, and the two older kids left the house with him. Gali, as was her habit, fought me tooth and nail about wearing her pink dress, which was in the laundry. When I told her it wasn't an option, she shrieked so loudly, I thought the neighbors would call child protective services on me. We finally compromised on a yellow dress with flowers. Gali asked if we could take the long route to school, and when she asks in her sweet voice, it's impossible to refuse her, so I agreed. On the way, we saw our neighbor Ruthi watering her plants. Gali waved hello, and I smiled, and then we ran into Matan and his father, Lior, who looked like he had been cut straight out of the pages of a fashion magazine, as usual. I stretched out my faded shirt to conceal the belly flab left over from my pregnancies, despite Gali already being three years old, and quietly cursed my sweatpants, which should have been tossed into the trash a long time ago.

Lior looked up and said, "Good morning to Gali's mother and to Gali. Matani, say good morning." He nodded his head with a friendly smile and Matan mumbled something. Gali smiled at him, and my throat closed up for a moment.

Stroking Gali's little head, I answered in a croaky voice, "Good morning, Lior. Gali's mother has a name, you know, and that name is Maya." Lior replied, "Good to know, Gali's mother, Maya." He held the door open for Gali and me and then for Matan, and I thought to myself that not only was he a casual supermodel, but also a gentleman. Then my mind switched over to Yairi, and I wondered if he was flirting with the mothers at the preschool or at work. I gave Gali a big kiss, swearing to myself that I would never again leave the house in the morning without a proper goodbye to Yairi, then I walked home quickly, praying that I wouldn't meet another familiar face. When I got inside, I was overwhelmed by the intense quiet, so much so that

I let it pleasantly sweep over me for a few minutes. Then I went into the bathroom and stood in front of the mirror to inspect myself—a woman in her late thirties, bags under her eyes, gray hairs overtaking the brown roots on her scalp. Soon, I was back at my computer and deep within the Russian forests, wondering where the hell I was going to take this story. How much pain could I bear to put down on paper? And to think I'd only just begun to describe their suffering. Back in the bathroom, I stood under the showerhead, the water cascading over my body, and I thought of the stark differences between my own comfort and the cruel cold of the Russian winter. I showered quickly and left the house, making sure I looked presentable this time around. Avishay scolded me for being late again, and as he and Dana were putting on their seatbelts, I hugged them both and said, "Let's go to McDonalds!" Dana shrieked, "Hooray!" and Avishay put on a fake frown, but he was clearly happy. And I thought how lucky it was that we'd decided to leave Gali in school until 4:00 p.m. that year, so the older ones could spend some quality time with me, too.

While we ate, Dana told us about her art teacher, who was teaching them how to paint portraits. When she said the word "portrait," I saw the same mannerism that Yairi used whenever he was excited about something, and I thought how blessed genetics can be sometimes, reminding us of what we love most about our loved ones, but sometimes it is also a curse, since we may not want to see a particular aunt suddenly reflected in one of our kids. I reminded myself to be attentive and not to let my mind migrate to its dusty corners. Dana told us how she "really really liked her teacher, Anat, for being the best teacher in the world," and I said, "Dana, now let's let Avishay tell us about his day." And Avishay said, "There was nothing special, really, just another day." Then he immediately asked, "*Ima*, how was your day?"

I was touched by his question, and tears welled up in my eyes. I replied that I'd written a bit and run some errands, but that the best part of my day was meeting them after school. They both tried to hide their proud smiles, and I was happy about the hour we'd spent together.

On the way home, I called the hair salon again and rebooked my appointment as well as an appointment for a facial—I couldn't even remember the last time I'd gotten one.

Chapter Thirteen: ITZHAK, SUMMER 1940

CAMP 19

That summer, we managed to put together a sort of routine. I liked to wake up early and help Mother bake bread from the durum flour we received. Father had already left early in the morning to forage for mushrooms, and sometimes he returned with forest fruits, or something else to boost our health and spirits. After everyone had risen and eaten their meager bread, I joined Father to fix odds and ends around the cabin, or anything else I could help do. Shimon did the same. Father went out to chop trees, like many in our camp, and when he returned in the evening, he was exhausted, but he did his best to help Mother out with anything he could. Then we would eat the meager bread once more, and when night finally fell, which was very late, we all conked out.

Shimon and I lugged the firewood, searched for plants that were edible or might have some medicinal use, and brought them to Mother. We also played with kids from the other families who had settled with us, all Jews just like us. I remember that summer well because at some point, I understood that Tzipke and I had become the leaders of the kids. We called our group "The Brave Bunch" since we were determined to help wherever we could and to pursue more daring operations in the forest. Of course, we also played hide and seek, buck buck, or any other game we imagined. We led all the kids, all of us hungry. We scavenged for berries and learned to identify edible mushrooms, which we collected and brought back for our parents to inspect. They were always happy to receive any fruit or vegetable that would enrich our feeble "menu," and we tried hard to keep the seams of our fraying pants together.

The days were long and pleasant; my family was together and that was the only thing that mattered. On Fridays, we gathered for a community *kiddush*. On Tisha B'Av, everyone fasted, including me—even though I was younger than eight years old—because I wanted to prove to Shimon that I was a man. He laughed and said he didn't see the use of fasting at my age since I'd have to do it for my whole life starting from when I turned thirteen, but I was stubborn and showed off my maturity, despite my nagging hunger. Mother saw how much I was suffering and offered me a piece of the durum bread, but I refused. At the end of the fast, we ate a few fruits that we'd foraged and finished off the day's durum bread. I was so proud of myself, and Grandpa said that I was really a man now. Seeing Shimon's wide smile, I knew that he was proud of me, too. That night, I went to bed with a slightly full belly, feeling a great amount of happiness and satisfaction. In the days that followed, I carried myself proudly, and all the kids pointed at me and whispered among themselves that I was the strongest kid in the entire camp. Tzipke looked at me with that look she got sometimes, I think it's the one that meant she was proud of me, and from that moment I felt like I still had so much more to prove.

***

2018

When I recall those moments today, my heart aches for that little boy who, with all his might, tried to prove that he was strong and capable, never admitting to any weakness, and I have concluded that his childhood was much too short.

I go downstairs for dinner, taking a seat next to Yaakov the Iraqi. We eat quietly and then head to the conference room, where a lecture has been scheduled for the evening: "South America: The Amazon Rainforest and Beyond." I sit attentively, fascinated by the speaker, who brims with confidence, and around whose kind eyes wrinkles sprout, produced by years of laughter.

"My trip into the Amazon was the journey of a lifetime," he begins. "Conquering the forest was a small victory for man, but his revelation that nature is eternal—an even greater one. If only you could have been there with me, you would have a clearer understanding of what I'm talking about." I look at him, and at the elderly people around me, all nodding their heads, and think about how my own life's journey had happened too early. I crossed rivers and lakes, facing frostbite and hunger—a traveler whose only objective was to survive another day—the growing hole in his stomach the main subject occupying his mind.

"The youngsters of today don't know what they're all about; they come to gloat about their travels without ever realizing that the journey is life itself." That's what I think to myself, and then I go back to listening. Looking around me, I notice that a few of the heads have begun to droop, eyes fluttering shut, while others are still listening intently, and I make an effort to steer my mind away from the Russian forests of the war. The eighty-six years I've lived have been far from simple, and the second World War may have been the longest of all the wars I endured; but it was also only the first, and unfortunately, not the last. I return to the child I once was and see him skipping among the trees of Russia's dense forests, listening for sounds of prowling night animals and for chirps of the morning birds. I return to my empty stomach and to the touch of my mother's hand, and then suddenly remember Tzipke, the girl I once loved, and I wonder what fate befell her. The lecture is over, and I make my way to the elevator, and from there to my room. Tonight, I'll fall asleep hoping I won't get lured back into my nightmares.

Chapter Fourteen: ICHU, SUMMER 1940

CAMP 19

At night, I heard them whispering. My dear aunt was burning up with a fever, and they had run out of ideas. Besides the herbal remedies my mother concocted, there were no medicines available. They made her tea from leaves we'd gathered, but she could barely bring her lips to the cup, and helplessness hung in the air. They even spoke with the guard, who sent them back angrily, saying he didn't have any answers for them. Mother whispered to Father to "keep quiet, and not worry Ichu," so I froze in bed, budging only to wipe my eyes, so that they wouldn't see the tears streaming down my face. Clutching the coin I always kept in my pocket, I forced myself to stay awake until everybody else had fallen asleep, and until Chasya, my beloved aunt, had stopped coughing.

When I woke up, nobody was in the cabin. Only those pesky flies that buzzed around restlessly. I didn't understand where everyone had gone. I looked at Chasya's bed. It was empty. I got up and ran outside, and there before me, Grandpa held Mother and my sisters held each other. When Father noticed me, he came over, placed his hand gently on my shoulder, and said, "The Lord gave and the Lord hath taken away; blessed be the name of the Lord."

"Father, what happened to Aunt Chasya?" I screamed, and the wails around me intensified. I released my father's grip and ran into the forest. Shimon ran after me, but I ran faster, not stopping until I knew that nobody was around. I fell to the ground and began sobbing. I loved Aunt Chasya so much; she used to laugh at everything that came out of my mouth and always snuck me a warm roll whenever I came to visit the bakery where she had worked. Aunt Chasya hadn't even had a chance to get married; she was only a bit older than Shimon, my brother; in fact, she was barely more than a girl. How was it possible that she was never coming back? I'd already seen what had happened to Shloime's grandmother, how she'd gone one day and never returned, and even though everybody thought Shloime didn't understand anything, he had admitted to me that she had died. He asked me not to say anything, maybe it was better for them to think he was a little boy who didn't understand anything; but a boy of seven-and-a-half already knows what it means to die. Nobody comes back from the place where the dead people go.

I lay on the ground for a few hours. I think I might've fallen asleep. When I woke up, it was almost dark. Fall had arrived, the days were getting shorter, I was cold and hungry, and then I heard my mother calling me in a concerned voice, "Ichu, Ichu, where are you, my baby?"

"I haven't been a baby for a long time," I said out loud, angry that they had buried Aunt Chasya without even telling me. And then I felt Mother's warm, loving arms reaching out toward me, hugging me, saying, "Come Ichu, let's go back to the cabin." I walked beside her, still wrapped in her embrace. When we got back, nobody asked any questions; only Father smiled at me, and I saw that Shimon was holding his tongue so as not to blurt anything out. When he was about to burst, Father gave him that special look of his that can silence anybody. Mother served me my meal, which was slightly bigger that day, and we all sat together, our clothes becoming more worn by the day, my beloved Aunt Chasya's seat empty.

I swore never to forget her, and I promised myself that from that day on, I would be more responsible, help Father even more, and I wouldn't cry even when I really needed to, because Shimon was right, I wasn't a baby anymore. Truth be told, I did end up crying a few more times in my life, but that is a separate story entirely.

Chapter Fifteen:
MAYA, 2019

TEL AVIV

When I opened my bedroom window this morning, I was greeted by the smells of spring and birds chirping a cheerful song, thankful for their final victory over the long, grueling winter. Last night was so humid. Although it isn't yet summer, a heat wave has already hunkered down on the Tel Aviv streets, turning everything annoyingly sticky. I wonder if it's a sign that summer will be longer and more treacherous than usual—I hope not.

Spring is my favorite season. The sun can be fickle at times, but after a day or two of unexpected rain, it never fails to come back out. The air is refreshing, and the winter wildflowers have not yet passed their prime. From our bedroom window, I can see a field of daisies down below, or at least the ones that have been spared the bulldozer's tires. On the way to Gali's preschool, there is always an assortment of wildflowers on display—a sight that always uplifts our spirits.

When I woke up, I snuggled closer to Yair, trying to wrap my arms around his neck; but he dodged me awkwardly, and said, "I'm in a rush today, Maya. Could you help me get the kids ready for school?" I didn't reply, only retreated back into myself, trying not to cry. Before he went to wake up the kids, Yair turned to me and said, "And if you have a couple minutes, maybe we should start planning our summer vacation? I thought maybe we could go to Holland." I replied that I wasn't sure we were fit to travel anywhere together, given the state of things between us. He mumbled, "I'm not sure what you want from me. If you don't want to plan anything then don't," and he went to the kids' room.

I heard him waking them up, and I knew that Avishay was pressing his head into his pillow and begging for five more minutes of sleep, while Dana had run immediately to the closet to look for the pink shirt I had bought her last week that had just come out of the laundry. Slowly, I got out of bed, went into the kitchen, boiled some water, turned on the coffee maker, found the rolls from yesterday with hummus for Avishay and cheese for Dana, and then the phone rang. On the other end, a woman said with a thick accent said, "Hello," and I replied, "Good morning," and she asked hesitantly if she was speaking with Maya Levin, and I said, "Who is asking?"

"My name is Tzipi Shmuelovitch," she said. "I received your number from your mother. We were on an organized trip for senior citizens together last week in Jerusalem." I listened to her voice and tried to imagine who this woman was and why she was calling me. "Your mother is a very nice woman," she added, and I smiled to myself, trying to remember if we'd planned a date to visit my parents soon.

"Thank you," I replied. Since when did my mother talk about me to people she had just met? What did this friendly old woman want from me?

"Your mother told me that you're doing some sort of research project about the Jews of Galicia, and I think I might be able to help you. Would you like to meet?"

"Could you give me a bit more information?" I asked.

She quickly replied, "Yes, of course. Look, your mother and I sat beside one another on the long bus ride to Jerusalem, and on the way back, too, and you know how it is, women like to talk, to share things with each other. Anyway, we started talking about my family, and your family, and your mother told me that you write stories documenting peoples' lives, and I must say, I was very impressed. So, I expressed my interest, and then she told me you are currently writing the story of somebody whose family was expelled from Poland to Russia at the beginning of the war. Well, when I heard that sentence my ears perked up, and you're probably wondering why." The woman was speaking so fast, I couldn't get a word in. "You see, my family and I were also expelled from Galicia by the Nazis."

As if anticipating her reply, I asked, "From where in Poland exactly were you expelled?" And something inside of me began to bubble up expectantly, and I almost blurted out, "I hope it was from Tarnobrzeg."

"You won't believe what I'm about to tell you," the woman continued. "I suggest you sit down, make yourself comfortable, on a chair or the couch, whatever it may be," she said dramatically, "Just take a seat."

My heart was pounding now, nearly about to burst, when she said, "Tarnobrzeg, Tarnobrzeg." Twice, she said it. I put down the phone to steady my breathing, then picked it up again to ask, "And the Ozer family—do you remember them?"

"Of course, I remember, how could I forget? You know, their family and my family were like two peas in a pod; we were neighbors and then expelled together, oh, there are too many stories to recount. I thought I could tell you about our journey, which is so intertwined with the Ozer's. Maybe hearing my story could help you with your writing, somehow."

I told her that I'd be happy to speak more, and we scheduled a meeting at a café close to the nursing home where the woman lived.

I didn't say anything to Yairi about the conversation. When the kids were ready for school, I kissed each of them on the cheek, hugged them, and wished them a wonderful day, then said goodbye to Yairi coldly, closed the door behind them, and went to get Gali ready for preschool, trying to calm the storm of thoughts that had descended on me. Was this woman's family really as close to the Ozer family as she claimed? Which details would I need to understand her story? Could this be the woman Itzhak had loved as a young boy? At record speed, I helped Gali get dressed and brushed her teeth and hair. Taking a shortcut, we bypassed the fields Gali loved to frolic in, and I promised to make it up to her when I picked her up in the afternoon. Outside the school, I saw Matan's father again, flashing that same snazzy magazine smile in his suave attire, and I wondered how it was possible that he didn't have a single white hair on his head or a wrinkle on his gorgeous face. He was older than me by a few years. Flustered, I walked by him, trying to focus on my meeting with Tzipi.

Tzipke.

The Tzipke? I wondered. How many Tzipkes could there have been in a small village like Tarnobrzeg, which hardly anyone had ever heard of. I called Yairi to tell him the good news since we had hardly seen each other in the morning. He answered via a text, saying he was in a meeting.

"Is it urgent?"

"Nothing urgent. Get back to me when you have a few minutes, there's something I wanted to tell you."

I skipped all the way back home, showered quickly, put on a blue button-down shirt, and over it a light gray jacket my mother had given me. After pinning up my loose hair, I set out for my meeting with Tzipke.

When I arrived a few minutes past nine, the café was full of people, and I quickly spotted an older woman waving at me from the corner. She had a wide, warm smile and was admirably put together. Her blonde hair was collected into a neat bun, her face was flatteringly made-up, and she wore a blue suit that accentuated her kind blue eyes. Aided by a cane, she rose to greet me, and shook my hand warmly.

"You're the spitting image of your mother. I recognized you at once," she said triumphantly, as if having proven to herself that old age couldn't stop her from making astute observations.

I smiled at her, while wondering how much our appearances truly reveal about our inner selves given how different my mother and I were. And if appearances were an accurate indicator, then I must have been in the presence of a very special woman, beautiful inside and out. I prayed silently, "Please let this be Itzhak's Tzipke."

We sat down and chatted about the nursing home where she had been living for the past few years, about the activities she pursued to help keep her healthy, both mentally and physically, and about her insistence on attending every one of the nursing home's outdoor excursions, despite her reliance on a cane.

"I know this country like the back of my hand, and still, on every trip, I discover new places and heroic tales from history." Tzipke ordered tea with lemon and I, a cappuccino, and when our order arrived, I felt as though I'd known her for many years already, and this was simply a routine meeting between old friends.

After we had exhausted the small talk, Tzipke asked me about my family, how many kids I had, boys or girls or both, and told me how much she had enjoyed my mother's company. I couldn't help think about the different personalities my mother put on for people who didn't know her versus for my sister and me. For a moment, I was struck by a deep sadness.

Then Tzipke said, "I'm so happy that you agreed to meet me on such short notice," and then lowered her blue eyes.

How beautiful she must have been in her youth. A wave of sorrow passed over me as I imagined life galloping toward its finish line so rapidly, mercilessly engraving its aging signs in all human beings. Straining a smile, I asked her to tell me about herself and about her relationship with the Ozer family. She told me that she would soon be celebrating her eighty-fifth birthday, wondering out loud how many more years she might have left. She'd heard from my mother—a "very pleasant woman," she emphasized again, and again my heart flinched—that I was looking for more material about the family. "I was moved," she said, "because I knew the Ozer family so well. Now I am here to tell you about them and to ask you some questions: What have you learned? Are they all in Israel? Are they even alive? And their children? Grandchildren?"

My mother, naturally, had not mentioned a thing about the woman sitting across from me; instead, she had divulged every detail about what she'd eaten on the trip and complained about the organizers. Knowing I was in the middle of a research project about this town, about Itzhak and his family, she had nevertheless chosen to speak about herself, and only herself.

"Our families were neighbors," Tzipke said as she stirred her tea, her eyes aglow. "The Ozer family and mine, we lived right next door to one another. Their parents were good people, and their grandfather, Grandpa Eli, was in many ways our grandfather as well. He essentially adopted us since our grandparents lived in the city, and we stayed in the village because my father was a Talmud teacher there. We had very tight neighborly relations; my mother, bless her soul, and Haya, Ichu's mother, that's what we called him when he was young, were the best of friends. They helped each other with everything—sometimes even the baking— dividing up the workload for Shabbat and the holidays; and if somebody was sick, Haya, who was a wizard with medicinal herbs, would come and take care of us. When we were in Siberia, in the forests, Haya saved people from death again and again. There were no doctors or hospitals, only the herbs she found and the remedies that she concocted." Tzipke became pensive as she collected her thoughts.

"You must understand," she continued passionately, "we were like their extended family, and I was almost Ichu's age, maybe a year or two younger, and we always played together, all the kids from the neighborhood, even the 'big ones' sometimes, mostly because Ichu's sisters Shifra and Sia were lovely girls with wonderful senses of humor, and they always invented new games, so we were never bored when we were together. And his brother Shimon," she added without taking a breath, "was always laughing at Ichu, but nice to me, and he made sure that

Ichu and I were on the same team whenever we split up for a game because he knew that his parents and mine had always discussed the possibility of our eventual marriage. Just so you know," she said, blushing, "Ichu didn't care that he was made fun of for playing with a girl."

"So, you are Tzipke," I said in amazement, now breathless myself. "The one and only."

"What do you mean?"

"The Tzipke, Ichu's best friend. He told me all about you," I said, and a wide smile broke across my face. I had been led to Itzhak's Tzipke effortlessly, so much so that she had found her way to me. Stunned, I looked at her and couldn't help thinking that sometimes life can surprise us even more than a soap opera. And that the dramas we experience couldn't be dreamed up in a script. Tzpike couldn't imagine how happy she had made me that morning.

From Itzhak's stories about Tzipke, I learned that she had gone to America, and since then, nobody had heard from her or any of her family members. Even when he visited America—Brooklyn in the seventies—he thought that maybe he would run into one of them on the street, maybe even her, but that didn't materialize. They disappeared as though the earth had swallowed them up. And I, too, thought that maybe I would look for her when the time was right, but lo and behold, the miracle had happened through my mother, from whom I hadn't expected a thing.

"He told you all about me?" Tzipke repeated, snapping me from my daydream.

"Yes." I nodded. "He told us that when you lived in Tarnobrzeg, you were together whenever you had the chance, anywhere, anytime. That the two families travelled together in Lvov after you were expelled from the village, and that afterward, you were both sent to the labor camp in Siberia."

"So," Tzipke said, inspecting her hands intently, at a loss for words, "it turns out he didn't forget about me." She fell silent for what seemed like a long time, and so did I.

Observing her tense body language, I said, "No, he didn't forget, and it appears that neither did you. But he also has no idea what happened to your family, what fate had in store for you. If I understand correctly, it seems like you don't know much about what happened to him, either."

Studying her face, I again found myself daydreaming about the meetings of Itzhak and Tzipke in their youth. I needed to plan how I would tell him about this meeting, and how I would arrange a reunion, given that his nursing home was in Jerusalem and hers in Tel Aviv.

When we regained our composure, Tzipke asked me to tell her about Ichu. I offered some brief details, including the fact that he lived in Jerusalem and wasn't very mobile, and that I hoped to reconnect them soon, if she was interested.

Tzipke blushed and replied, "Of course, I'd like that. When do you think it might be possible?"

I told her I would check with him and get back to her, and then I asked her to tell me a bit more about what she had gone through during the war. She was quiet for a moment, and then began speaking about the first days of the war, when the Nazis took over their village and terrorized it, and then about the rounding up of the Jews in the village square; the humiliating expulsions, after which they were destitute; about Mother Russia, her life in Lvov, and that her most vivid memories from the war were the terrible losses, freezing temperatures, and constant hunger. I asked about what had happened after the families left the forest, where they went, and she replied that her parents had chosen a different path from that of Ichu's family, leaving her to wonder what had become of them, and whether their lives had been less difficult. Finally, she said that she sometimes thought about her parents and the unimaginable tragedies that befell them, and she wondered how they had survived such loss not only during the war, but also afterward. I didn't ask her to elaborate. I didn't want to cause her more pain.

"Based on what Itzhak told me, your family went to America after the war."

"Yes and no," Tzipke said. "That was the original plan, but there ended up being a problem with the visa to America, so we sailed to Canada and lived there for a few years, until my uncle, who had emigrated to Brooklyn before the war, managed to get us visas to come over."

"Itzhak didn't know any of that," I told her.

"We sent letters, but we didn't hear anything back, except for rumors that they had made Aliyah. We thought maybe they had forgotten us," she said. "The friendship between the families—we thought it would last forever, and we couldn't imagine back then that we might not see them again. It was difficult for all of us, especially for my mother, who loved Itzhak's mother Haya like a sister, and for me, it was difficult because I hoped and dreamed that he would look for me, and we would get married." Tzipke blushed and continued, "Look, until that cursed war came along, we lived a happy village life, and when the Nazis entered our village, our lives were torn to shreds. Nothing ever returned to how it was before, and after the war, we were all broken, and each of us went our own way."

She was silent, and I didn't say a word. Despite seeing that she was in pain, I finally asked her to tell me more about the war, and she agreed, saying that she'd prepared for this conversation ahead of time, and that it was okay; but just so that I was aware, despite the passing of more than seventy years, the memories of the war were often as visceral as though they had occurred yesterday. Silently, we sipped from our mugs, and then she said quietly but intently, "I'll never forget the day of the expulsion." And a shadow of bitter fear bore into her eyes.

"We had already felt terror in the streets for a few weeks. The Nazis were approaching, and the Poles didn't spare us the evil in their hearts and their hatred of Jews. The atmosphere was violent all around, but the day we were told to drop everything and gather in the center of the village was the worst of all. My parents took me and my three brothers, I was only five or six, and despite my young age, I remember the day's events very well. The youngest of us was less than a year old, and Mother packed a small bag for us with a few sweaters, rags for diapers, and a bit of milk for the baby, and we went to the center of the village. Mother was afraid they would shoot us, so she told us to not utter a sound, and you'll be surprised to hear that everybody, even baby Shloime, was completely silent until we reached the river after an exhausting walk. Then he began to scream, and Mother tried to nurse him, but he refused and kept screaming; and then a Nazi came and just grabbed him from her arms and flung him into the river. Mother fainted, and we were too afraid to utter a peep, so we cried silently.

"Israel Ozer, Ichu's father, saw us standing there and immediately moved us to the side to help us cross the river with his family. He saved our lives. Mother didn't speak for a few days, she only cried, and Father told her to focus her attention on us, that there was no time to mourn, but I saw that he was having a hard time, too. We were lost amidst all the chaos. We didn't know where we were going or what would become of us, but I wanted to make my brothers laugh, to keep them occupied, despite my many worries."

Tzipke fell silent again. Wiping a tear from the corner of my eye, I looked at her, but said nothing. She continued. "We eventually found ourselves in Lvov with them. Did he tell you about Lvov?" I nodded, recalling how they had lived in the rubble of ruined buildings for a few weeks. Tzipke smiled and said, "Once, Ichu, his sister Sima, and I decided to venture into the forest on our own when our parents were out looking for something to eat, and we got lost and couldn't find our way home."

"He told me," I nodded, though I didn't remember Ichu mentioning Tzpike in that story. At that moment, there was a mischievous, childish look in her eyes. "We were little rascals, and certain that we knew the way back home, but of course, that wasn't the case. We wandered the streets for a few hours, walking in circles, until we finally asked somebody to help us using the street corner names we remembered; the stranger helped us and took us home. Afterward, we didn't dare go on any more adventures like that one, and in any case, a few weeks later we were told to pack our bags, and we were loaded onto the trains that took us to Russia."

Tzipke paused, finished her tea, and said that they were with the Ozer family in the forest, too, but that afterward they were separated from each other. Her pale cheeks reddened. "My parents, after two years of living together in the camp, decided that we would leave whenever it became possible, and that's what we did; we walked right out of there and walked for weeks, until we arrived at a village named Joreina, where we stayed until the end of the war. My father was able to find work with some rich man who had a large piece of land and needed working hands, and he gave us a shelter. The Ozer family stayed behind in the camp." Tzipke looked up at me, and I saw her pure heart peering out again, but also a deep sadness that I hadn't noticed earlier; I was hit by another wave of gratitude that the meeting was even taking place.

I thought about how lucky my family was to live in a gated community and gainfully employed, to eat a warm meal every night and able send our children off to school every day. I reminded myself to appreciate these things even more than I currently did, to appreciate the protective bubble in which I lived, which kept me and my children safe and secure.

Tzipke suddenly smiled and said, "Did Ichu tell you that we learned how to hunt bears in the forest?"

"Hunt bears? No, he didn't. Maybe he hasn't gotten to that part yet." I smiled back at her. "How did you learn to hunt bears?"

"You know, when we were in the camp, Ichu and I rounded up a group that we called 'The Brave Ones.' It was composed of the bravest kids in the camp. We gathered everyone together and went on all sorts of daring missions. We must have been seven or eight years old, some of us maybe nine or ten, no more, but with our life experience, we thought of ourselves as at least sixteen." Tzipke laughed and waved her hand dismissively, and I could suddenly see her emerging from the past in all her radiance.

She continued. "When we lived in the forest, my parents were always busy with work—it was a labor camp, after all—and we didn't have too much to do during the day. One time, we helped an old lady carry some of her belongings, sometimes we helped our parents pick mushrooms in the forest—we became true experts when it came to picking the most delicious mushrooms, which saved us in the summer from the worst hunger. We also went on more serious missions. One of them required us to follow the Maris and learn how to hunt a bear. The Maris were natives, these big, scary people who everybody feared, but they didn't harm a soul, when it came down to it."

Then she said, "So one day we decided to really follow them to see how they hunted a bear. It was Ichu's idea, of course," Tzipke smiled, and her eyes glistened. "It was a one-of-a-kind mission. You don't get to see such a thing happen every day." Her face suddenly assumed a devious expression. "The Maris were excellent hunters, and for a good reason—all of their food came from the forests in which they lived, including the bears that they hunted for their furs to keep them warm in the harsh winters. It was the only meat available, so the Maris hunted, while we Orthodox Jews ate only plants and durum, which were small pellets that our parents ground up to make flat bread that satisfied no one's hunger, which was one of the reasons we were so weak and hungry. Many people died like flies there, but that's another story. Let's get back to the bears."

Chapter Sixteen: ICHU, NOVEMBER 1940

CAMP 19

Over the summer, the barbaric Maris taught me how to hunt a bear. Not just any bear, but a black bear, the really scary kind that you don't want to ever meet in the middle of the forest. Snakes are actually much scarier to me than bears. Snakes peer out from the ground when you least expect it. And then they bite you. Their venom can be poisonous, and they scare me like crazy.

So how do you hunt a bear? I know the answer since I followed the Maris, who are some of the biggest natural heroes I've ever known. They're huge, with big mouths and usually only one or two teeth, and the truth is that meeting somebody like that in the middle of the night, that caveman type, is a dubious experience. The Maris were actually very friendly toward us, my family and me, and I wasn't afraid of them at all. I even became friends with one of the kids. His name was Roar, and he was a little younger than me. Sometimes, we jumped in puddles together and foraged red berries in the forest. He could always point out what was edible and what was not, and Father allowed me to go with him because he trusted that if an animal suddenly pounced on us, Roar would know what to do. Father knew that the Maris were the kings of the forest, and they taught their children to blend into nature from a young age.

But let's get back to the black bear hunt. So, how did I know how to hunt a bear? An excellent question. My learned wisdom came from the Maris, and it's all quite fascinating and simple, but mostly simple. The Maris fish for a specific kind of fish in the Volga River. It has a flexible bone that looks like a spring. They round out the bone then add prongs made of sharp pieces of stone, which they stick into a lump of frozen fat. They make a lot of balls like that, since the bears love to eat fat and are attracted to the smell. It all takes a long time, both the fishing and the ball-making, but the Maris have a lot of patience, because they don't seem to be rushing anywhere in particular. I think patience is of the utmost importance when trying to hunt a bear.

The Maris gather all their equipment and go out to search for bears. They spend a lot of time looking for tracks, and there are days when they don't even come across fresh ones, and then there's no point in leaving the fat mixture filled with the bones and prongs. When they do finally come across fresh footprints, they scatter the stinky stuff right over them. But it gets even more interesting. The bear swallows the ball, and when the fat heats up inside its belly, the fishbone expands, tearing his stomach—at least, that's what I understood from Roar and his father, who is a big expert in hunting bears. After swallowing the ball, the bear and his steps become heavy, and he slows down as he starts to feel sick. That's the perfect time for the Maris to jump out and trap him, easy as one-two-three. Whenever they catch a bear, they throw a big party at which they stab the sleepy animal with sharp knives and begin to strip his skin.

Then they eat the bear meat. Believe me, when I tell you that it's a gruesome sight, and I've tried to wipe it from my memory.

Roar told me they also sell the warm bear fur to whoever pays the most. We Jews don't eat bear meat, and honestly, haven't eaten any meat at all since leaving Poland, since we keep kosher. We make do with our durum porridge, and with the berries and mushrooms we forage, which is why I am hungry most of the time. Sadly, we don't have the means to buy the warm furs from the Maris, so in the wintertime we are very, very cold.

I saw the Maris making their bone-fat mixture and hiding it in all sorts of places plenty of times, but I only saw them during the hunt once. I have to say, it was quite exciting, if also a little scary, since it's strange to see people hunting large bears. I was really afraid of the bears. Father had warned me that when walking through the forest, I should always make noise, so that the bears know somebody is in there with them because the truth is that bears, however big and scary, are just as afraid of us as we are of them, and rightfully so. The Maris put out traps for them, skinned them, and ate their meat, so the bears, if they detected any noise, knew to keep their distance, unless it was a particularly aggressive bear, but luckily, I never came across one of those.

It was a bright summer day when I witnessed the bear hunt. The Maris were roaming around not far from our cabins, checking if the traps they'd left the day before had been set off. One of them shouted at another, and based on the joy spread across his face, I understood that he'd noticed a missing trap. I began to follow them, not by myself, of course. I had filled my sister Sima and Tzipke in on the mission. They were just as curious as I was, and I'd sworn them to secrecy, making them promise not to tell our parents, obviously, and not even Shifra or Shimon, who would be angry, too. And that's how, quietly, we began to follow the Maris as they checked for tracks. It hadn't rained in a few days, but it was still pretty easy to see any imprints in the ground, which was damp most days of the year.

After wandering in circles for a while, they stopped. From a distance, we saw that they'd spotted something, and I hoped it was really a bear. It walked slowly, carrying itself with great difficulty, and the ambush commenced. They shot arrows at the bear, shouting words I didn't understand, and then it simply toppled over, and they attacked it with knives until it was completely dead. Tzipke was on the verge of letting out a scream. To avoid a disaster, I went over to her and covered her mouth, telling her to turn around and close her eyes, and then I looked at Sima, who until that point hadn't let a word escape from her mouth, and I understood that if we didn't head back to the cabins at once, things could take a wrong turn.

Clasping their shoulders, I told them that we had to go back to the cabin, and as I spoke, I had to accept that we wouldn't be sticking around for the skinning. Before she could respond, a wave of vomit exploded from Sima's mouth. So that's why she hadn't spoken. Trying not to throw up myself, I led the three of us back to the cabin, where we remained. Since then, we didn't witness any more hunts, because even though it was exciting, it was also brutal seeing a big, beautiful black bear being murdered. To think about what happened afterward is even more horrifying, so we decided, the three of us, Tzipke, Sima, and I, not to tell anyone, and not to follow the Maris anymore. It was enough to understand the process, and we really admired those savage hunters. If they could overcome bears in the wild, they could overcome anything, because they were the great masters of nature, while we were just a thin and tired bunch who lived on durum bread, herbs, mushrooms, and berries, when we got lucky.

Chapter Seventeen: ITZHAK, 2019

JERUSALEM

I don't feel well tonight. My stomach churned with sharp spasms, and I knew that my intestines were blocked and that I would need to go to the hospital where they would insert a painful IV tube into my nose, release the obstruction, and I'd start a slow recovery, just like last time. I decide to wait until morning, so as not to bother my daughter and her husband. The night was endless, and I couldn't sleep, or even move, since each movement caused the next to be more painful. Morning will soon be here, and then I'll call them, I decide. At a certain point, I thought about the hunger I'd experienced as a child compared to the abundance of today, the gluttony, and all those restricted foods, the "enemies," that's what I call them; but we only live once, and after those years of scarcity, even today, in my advanced age, it's hard to know when to stop eating because maybe one day I will be hungry again and there won't be even a morsel around. There are days when I keep at it until my stomach is about to explode. My wife used to look away when that happened.

Those years in the Russian forests were difficult. On the one hand, we experienced cold and hunger, and we weren't free, which is a horrible thing to be a prisoner always fearing the prospect of punishment. On the other hand, we weren't treated too unfairly, and it was wartime, which meant we weren't the only ones suffering. Most people in Europe were experiencing some kind of shortage at the time, not to mention the six million Jews who had been murdered at the hands of the Nazis, may their memory be a blessing. I lay there and thought about all those things, and about how we didn't understand back then that what we went through in the forest was nothing compared to what we'd endure after being released from the camp.

For our duration in the camp, the Russians used the Jewish inmates as woodcutters. My father, Israel, was the liaison between the two groups. He spoke a bit of Russian but communicated mainly through his warm smile. He was seen as a strong leader, physically and mentally, and was trusted to carry out orders in the best manner possible. The logs we chopped were lugged to the river, where they were led by the current to the wood factory in the nearby town. That is how we lived until June 1941.

On June 22, 1941, Germany advanced into the Soviet Union unannounced, despite the Molotov-Ribbentrop Pact, named after the countries' ministers of foreign affairs and signed in August 1939. The pact declared a decade-long peace. Perhaps as a result of their surprise, the Soviet Union decided to release us from the labor camp. We didn't know what to do. Should we look for a better place to live? What happens when prisoners get used to the lack of freedom in their daily lives, so difficult, yet familiar? The camp manager suggested that Father look for lodging in the nearby town and keep chopping wood, but Mother claimed that the physical demands would do him in, and on top of it all, the sanitary conditions in the labor camp were unfit for living: extreme cold, hunger, mosquitos, and disease. Out of the thousand who had arrived, only half of us remained. My lovely aunt had died in this camp, like so many others, and Mother wanted to get away from this place that reminded her of so much suffering. My grandpa put an end to the debate. During World War I, he had arrived in Astrakhan at the foot of the Volga River. He told us that the city had been beautiful, and that despite the widespread hunger plaguing the Soviet Union at the time, the place appeared overflowing with abundance, as if the war was a fiction. Grandpa thought the same thing was probably happening now, that the areas far from the frontlines were the ones where scarcity would be least felt. When the members of our community heard what Grandpa Eli had to say, they decided to join us on our journey.

Chapter Eighteen: MAYA, 2019

TEL AVIV

When I left the café, the sun was already in the center of the sky. I walked to the car, double-checked that my recording had been saved, and thought about how I'd only get to listen to it after the weekend since Yairi's birthday was on Saturday.

I decided not to tell Itzhak about the meeting over the phone, but in person, which I knew would delight him, and I prayed that I would be able to finish the book while he was still alive. With his old age and teetering health, he was hanging on by a thread. He had leukemia, was blind but for the shadows he saw from the corners of his eyes, and deaf beyond what his handy hearing aid provided; but above all, he was an old man who had lived a hard life. My writing had become a race against time. I promised myself to visit Itzhak in his nursing home as soon as possible after Yairi's birthday celebrations. I would take him to a café, tell him about Tzipke, and ask if he would like to speak to her on the phone, or perhaps get together in person. The phone rang—it was Yairi, and from the first sound, I knew that he was stressed, and I should make it short. "Nothing urgent," I said. "I wanted to tell you that I met Itzhak's first love, the one I told you about, who he saw for the last time in the displaced persons camp."

"Very nice. Congratulations. How did you find her?"

"You won't believe it, but my mother actually did. I'll tell you the rest of the story in the evening."

When I hung up the phone, I felt a nagging distress. It erupted from inside of me, unrelated to Yairi, my mother, Itzhak, Tzipke, or anybody else in the world. Itzhak's story had taken a significant twist, and so had mine. I needed to navigate my work and children, and Yairi wasn't there for me anymore. Were these the circumstances in which I wanted to grow old?

Still, I went to the Ayalon Mall to buy Yairi a new shirt and a wallet since his old one was falling apart. I started to plan his birthday, putting my own needs aside once again, but this time I vowed to check in with myself afterward. It was long overdue to give myself some attention. I thought about which cake I would bake for my husband, called his parents and invited them to lunch on Saturday, and hoped that Yairi would appreciate it. I also called my sister and told her what had happened with Tzipke; at least she had the patience and energy to listen to me, even enthusiastically. I reminded her that Yairi's birthday was coming up and asked her, if she had time to spare, to organize a game to keep the children occupied. Then I called my mother and tried to stay calm, but the minute I mentioned Tzipke she complained that I "always had something mean to say to her" and that I should just thank her for connecting me with the woman. I stopped myself from slamming down the receiver, feeling guilty about my pent-up anger. After cutting the conversation short, I breathed deeply, deeply and slowly, until I was entirely out of air, and then I put on Beethoven's Seventh Symphony and cranked up the volume. After a few minutes, the world looked a bit brighter.

I went to pick up the kids. When they got into the car, I felt as though life had returned to its regular rhythm. Dana told me that when Yarden, a boy, joined the school choir, everyone laughed at him, but she thought that it was very cute, especially since he didn't care what people said about him. She said, "It's not only for girls, just like tae-kwon-do isn't only for boys." Avishay nodded and said, "Singing and dancing is for boys, too." I almost stopped the car and turned around to give them both a huge hug.

Looking at them from the rear-view mirror, I thought about how my love was limitless, unbound, and how I was so lucky to have such wonderful children, and then they began to fight again over the girl-boy conundrum and who was meant to play soccer. Avishay claimed, "Boys are stronger, and girls are crybabies," while Dana fumed and said, "Not all girls are crybabies, and they can play soccer even better than the boys." And the sweet moment passed swiftly. When we got home, I gave them a snack and helped them with their homework. Then I went to pick up Gali from preschool. I marched right in there, grabbed her hand, and marched right out, brushing aside the teacher and informing her that I was in a rush, even though she was trying to tell me something. Once you get her talking, that teacher never stops, and I had neither the mental energy nor the time—I'd left the kids alone at home, and I had to get back.

On the drive home, my mother called and said that she'd thought about our earlier phone call, which had been "extremely unpleasant." I asked her why she hadn't told me about Tzipi, and she replied that she hadn't thought it was of any particular importance, and besides, she'd given her my phone number. I restrained myself from screaming but reminded her that she had no problem telling me in great detail about her colonoscopy from two weeks ago, but when it came to something that was important to me, she suddenly "forgot" to mention it. My stomach turned inside-out as I explained how I felt. My mother was silent, and then said, "You know, Maya, I don't know what's gotten into you, but you've changed. Check yourself, you're irritable and insufferable." She hung up without giving me a chance to respond. It was the first time in my life that I realized the only thing that interested my mother was herself, and nobody else, not even the elderly and their life stories. From the back seat, Gali said, "*Ima*, can I have a chocolate pudding when I get home?" Fighting off my tears, I gushed, "Of course, dear, of course, you can."

Chapter Nineteen: ITZHAK, JUNE 1941

LEAVING CAMP 19

One bright day in June 1941, we gathered up the few belongings we still had and started walking. Tzipke's family had left two weeks earlier, while my family debated whether to stay or to go since Kochak had promised my father that if we stayed, we would receive an extra daily serving of durum. It was a tempting offer, provoking many heated arguments, but we eventually resolved to leave. We walked in a group of eleven, our destination being Astrakhan, which was far from the border.

Grandpa had a vivid memory of Astrakhan from his time as a soldier in the first World War. The city had been unscathed by the war, and Grandpa was dazzled by it, which is why he suggested going back. The last weeks had been punctuated by the echoes of war creeping toward us, and I remember nights of fear spent curled up in my mother's arms. Beyond the sound of cannons, which scared my parents and me, there were also looming signs that we would be hungrier than before, which made our migration all the more urgent.

When we left the camp, it was the first time we had felt free since arriving in the Soviet Union. The Russians informed us that although we were not legal residents, we could travel wherever we wanted in Russia; in practice, they made us register every time we arrived in a new place, but we were lucky to be kept away from war zones with the claim that we were Jews, Polish refugees, and thus "unfaithful to the regime." I remember Mother saying she felt that we were going to be much better off now without anybody to boss us around, and Father smiling at her and telling us that we were on some sort of family trip in honor of Mother Russia—that was how we should think of the journey. I thought maybe now we would have more food since I was hungrier than ever, but the day after we reached the train station and stood in line, we received the same meager serving of durum which left a hole in our stomachs. Still, the glimmer of hope was no less important than our empty bellies.

The train rumbled on for a few hours, and in the afternoon, we arrived at a busy train station. We got off, wondering where to continue from there, thinking we should maybe even retrace our steps and return to where we came from. My aunt Gail insisted on the village closest to our camp, Yoshkar-Ola, where her husband Moshe was in the hospital. She had regretted joining us the moment we got on the train. Mother agreed to Yoshkar-Ola since Father had been so unsure about the trip to begin with.

When we got off at the stop, we looked around us, wondering what to do. To our surprise, we saw Noah, who was engaged to my aunt Rachel. Noah had been sent to a separate labor camp, and my aunt was sure that she wouldn't see him until the end of the war, or maybe ever again. Noah was thin, tired, and unshaven. We all ran toward him, and he raced toward us in disbelief. We embraced, drowning in our emotions, and Noah and Rachel cried. Afterward, Noah told us that he couldn't handle the torturous work in the labor camp any longer. He was sure that if he stayed there, he wouldn't last, so he'd waited for a moment when the guards were distracted and escaped. He jumped onto a train, praying that it would take him as far away as possible, never considering for a moment that he would be reunited with Rachel, the love of his life, whom he had missed so terribly, praying for her welfare, and that one day they would be together again. He couldn't have imagined their reunion would be so quick to come.

Noah appeared to be in distress. He explained that he was afraid the police would find out that he didn't have any papers, and if he got caught, he would be severely punished for running away from the camp. He asked Rachel if she'd be willing to present herself to the Russian soldiers as his wife if the need arose. Before Rachel could reply, Grandpa Eli said, "She doesn't need to pretend, she can actually become your wife, if you both agree to it."

Rachel and Noah gazed at one another, still unable to wrap their heads around their good fortune. Perhaps it wasn't exactly how they had pictured the most important day of their lives, but the prospect of separation was so terrifying that the couple couldn't think of anything they wanted more than to get married, right then and there. But how would they do it? Grandpa Eli assured them that they needn't worry, he would arrange everything.

Grandpa disappeared for a few minutes and returned with a ring that he borrowed from one of the women who'd been on the train with us. While four men held a piece of cloth above Noah's and Rachel's heads, Noah recited a blessing and slipped the ring onto Rachel's finger, trembling with excitement. What were the odds of them meeting here, at a crossroads, on the very day we'd left the labor camp? What were the chances that Noah would manage to escape from his own labor camp on the exact same day, hop on the first train, and arrive at the same destination as ours?

"*Harei, at mekudeshet li kedat Moshe ve Yisroel*," recited Grandpa Eli. Noah repeated after him, followed by, "*Im Ishkachech Yerushalaim, Tishachech Yemini*." We all stood around the new couple. Not a single eye was dry. Then the ceremony was over, and Rachel and Noah were married. They held each other tightly, afraid of what would happen if they let go for even a second.

At the end of the ceremony, it was decided that Rachel and Noah would accompany my aunt Gail back to Yoshkar-Ola, while we continued on to Astrakhan. We boarded a train that took us deep inside the landmass, as far as we could possibly get from the roaring of cannons, hoping and praying that an easier life awaited us. Of course, we also hoped that the echoes of war wouldn't reach Yoshkar-Ola. We didn't imagine it would take so many years to see them again, only to be separated once more when Gail, Noah, and Rachel immigrated after the war to faraway America, while we made Aliyah to Israel—but I'm getting ahead of myself again.

Chapter Twenty:
ICHU, JUNE 1941

Over the summer, when the adults decided that it was time to leave the labor camp, which had become my home, I wasn't sure I wanted to leave. I had a daily routine, I played with the other kids—and there were lots of kids to play with all the time. But the adults said that we were leaving on some kind of journey to a "really beautiful" city, and I thought to myself that maybe it wouldn't be so bad to move on. "The Brave Kids" had broken up, some of my family had already left, and Tzipke's family, too, and I didn't know where they had gone.

When Tzipke's family left, I tried to put on a stoic face and appear mature, as though I couldn't care less that they were leaving. But Tzipke could read me well. She saw that it was hard for me and promised that we'd meet again soon. I believed her and said that when we met again, we could get our old gang together and set out on some new missions. Smiling, Tzipke replied that she was up for anything, other than following barbarians and watching them hunt. I smiled back because I didn't want it to be hard for her, either, and I promised that I would keep my coin safe until our reunion, and that maybe after the war was over, we could buy an ice cream with it. Tzipke was the only one who knew about my coin. It was our secret.

When Tzipke was gone, and the others with her, I didn't really care as much whether we stayed or left and thought that maybe we'd even arrive at a nicer place. Father described the city we were going to, and it sounded okay. I hadn't visited any cities besides Lvov and Krakow, so maybe this place would have some charm to it, and maybe there would be enough food so that Father wouldn't have to work as hard as he had in the camp—at least, that's what Mother hoped. We packed up our few belongings, said a nice goodbye to all our friends who were staying behind, and went to the train station. All I could think about was that I would never again see my Mari friend, Roar, who came to play with me sometimes. I hoped that he wouldn't be too sad. Maybe he'd find another white friend who would be nice to him, at least as nice as I was. Roar had promised never to forget me, and I saw that he was having just as hard a time with our separation as I was. I didn't cry, but I think that he did, a little, because I saw a drop in the corner of his eye; but maybe it was something else, I'm not sure.

Whatever happened, I promised Roar that he was my best friend in the whole camp, that thanks to him I had done things I'd never dreamed of. Roar proposed a blood pact. At first, I didn't understand what he meant, but when it hit me, I panicked. What kind of barbaric custom was that? I told him we Jews didn't do blood pacts, that it went against our tradition, and while I respected his, he had to respect mine as well. Roar didn't argue, and I wasn't sure he got what I was saying, but we separated with a friendly handshake, which I had showed him how to do. Then, absorbed in my thoughts, I caught up with my mother, who told me to "watch where I was walking," as I almost fell into a huge puddle. Mother pulled me toward her, stopping me from splashing straight into it.

We kept walking like that for a long time. I was already very hungry and tired, but I didn't say a word since Shimon kept looking at me, and I knew that he was thinking I would soon start crying or complaining that I was hungry, so I didn't say anything and kept walking in silence. When we arrived at the train station, there was a long line for bread rations. With our ration slips, we stood for maybe ten hours, and I wanted to cry so badly, but finally our turn came, and my hunger was put on hold. Afterward, I ran after Mother to the train car that took us away from Yoshkar-Ola, and as soon as the train departed, I heard Aunt Gail tell Mother that she couldn't believe she had left her sick husband Moshe behind in the hospital.

Aunt Rachel had a grave expression on her face, and Mother told her that when we got to the next stop we'd simply turn around and ride back to Yoshkar-Ola; it didn't matter how hard Father would have to work there, it was better than nothing. But the train kept on going and going and the ride seemed endless, until we arrived at a stop and suddenly saw Noah, my aunt Rachel's fiancée, only he was thin and bald—I could barely recognize him. It was a big celebration, and we all cried, and then Grandpa suddenly said they should get married, so everybody cried even more. I swear, sometimes I don't get the grown-ups. They cry when things are bad, and they cry when things are good. At least I only cry when I feel bad and don't confuse my joy and sorrow. Then Noah and Rachel got married, everybody cried again, and I looked at Shimon and showed him how dry my eyes were. Even though I saw him shed a tear, I didn't dare tease him about it because it really was a happy moment after such a long difficult and sad time. We were quiet and that was all, but I must say, I found the whole affair quite funny.

Afterward, everybody began to argue about what to do next: Should we go back to Yoshkar-Ola or continue on to Astrakhan? I hoped that Astrakhan would win, since I wanted to go to the city Grandpa had described so magically in his stories. We eventually decided to part ways, with Aunt Gail, Rachel, and Noah on one train, and the rest of us on the other.

When we got moving again, it was already nighttime, and we were all very tired. After many days of travelling, we reached the Volga River, which I'd never seen before. I was curious to see if it really was as wide as I'd been told, and the answer was yes, it was indeed. The river was simply enormous! I couldn't make out the beginning or end of it from either direction.

When we reached the river, we got off the train and stood in line again for bread, which took a long time, but finally, our turn came, and Father told us only to nibble so that something would stay in our stomachs before we finished digesting. I was so hungry that I didn't even smile, but I did try to eat as slowly as I could, even though after a few moments, I realized I was still hungry. I decided not to say anything since I knew that Mother would sacrifice her own bread for me without a second thought. Sima had already explained to me that my mother needed to eat just as much as I did, and Shifra, who is usually quite the joker, always looked at me with disappointment whenever I asked for more, and that's a look I definitely didn't like getting, so I stayed hungry and silent.

Chapter Twenty-One: MAYA, 2019

TEL AVIV

In the evening, I told Yair, "I know myself, and the fact that I recorded and saved the interviews with Itzhak doesn't mean that I'll remember where to find them, so it's best that I just deal with them now, once and for all." He nodded and went back to his own affairs. I went to my study, turned on the tape, and started to transcribe it.

The meeting with Tzipke had raised so many thoughts and questions: Can love truly be eternal? Is it possible to love someone your whole life, even if you haven't seen them for decades? What does it feel like to love somebody for so many years without knowing whether they're dead or alive, or if they even remember you? Yair didn't ask me anything about the conversation with Tzipke, and the crater that had formed between us kept expanding. What was I to do? I didn't know the answer to that difficult question, or whether I should reach out for help. What I did know is that I was sinking into my own life, composed of a storm of unruly emotions, triggered by Itzhak and Tzipke's story as well as my husband's disinterest in me. I missed Yairi, who now lived beside me, instead of with me. I wanted so badly for him to take me into his arms.

It had gotten late. I found myself staring at the television for an hour, not processing any of it. I got up from the couch, turned off the lights, checked that the door was locked, and went upstairs. When I was about to open the bedroom door, I heard whispering and wondered who Yairi could be speaking to at such an hour. I opened the door and heard him say in an entirely different voice, "Okay, Moti, we'll speak more tomorrow. It's already late. Have a good day over there in Silicon Valley."

I went into the bathroom without saying anything, but as I brushed my teeth, I asked nonchalantly, "So, what's up with Moti? Are they coming back to Israel over the summer?"

Yair quickly replied that they were still deciding, and if they didn't visit this summer, they'd definitely come the next. I put on my pajamas and got into bed, pressing into Yairi's warm body, which he could never resist. When I reached for his cheek, he turned his back to me. Tonight, like last night, I wouldn't receive the embrace I so longed for. Tears streamed down my face. Within a minute or two, Yairi had fallen asleep, and I kept crying, for my own life, for that of my family, and for the entire Ozer family, whom I had left struggling yet again in Siberia. I thought how lonely we all were, each to their own, and that even when we brought others into our intimate circles, we weren't always able to talk to them, tell them how we truly felt, and that every family was lonely in its own way.

As these thoughts weighed on me, I promised myself I wouldn't become a victim. Tomorrow I would find a therapist with whom I could speak freely about my situation. The kind of therapist who wouldn't know anything about me or my family, other than whatever I told her, which meant that it would remain between us, and she would be on my side, period. The tears stopped flowing, and my head cleared.

Grandma Matilda, my father's mother, had once told me, "The heart wants what it wants, and there's nothing we can do about it." She was always full of love and admiration, always proud of me, and thought that I was the greatest miracle the world had ever received. Grandma Matilda gave big hugs and huge kisses, and her cookies couldn't be beat. No matter how many times my mother tried to bake them, they never made the cut. Grandma always offered practical advice. "Why would you ever hide your face with that gorgeous mane of hair?" I suddenly remembered how I'd taken Yairi to Grandma before introducing him to my parents.

"The one you brought this time is the most suitable for you out of all your suitors," she had said from her seat in the living room, inspecting Yairi and winking at him mischievously. "Don't play any games with him like you did with the others; you've got the golden ticket in your hands, and that's not something you want to lose." I remember looking at her, at Yairi, and knowing she was right. That heart, that tender, sensitive heart, needed to be nurtured, tucked into bed, in the hope that one day some of his goodness might stick to me. I always thought of Yairi as a much better person than me, the kind who knows how to be a true friend, who would love me through thick and thin, in sickness and in health, in youth and in old age, ugly as it may be. In those moments, I missed my grandma and her warm, encompassing embrace, and focused on the memory of her essence, hoping to channel her into my dreams that night.

At a certain point, I guess I fell asleep, and then the "great storm" ensued. Dana ran to me, crying that she had dreamt "something horrible." I asked her what it was, and she said that Alma and

Shay were giving her the silent treatment and didn't want to come to her birthday party. "They were so horrible, Ima, they laughed at me and said that dolls were for babies, but I think dolls are forever, right?" I looked at her sleepy face, calmed her down and said that of course dolls were forever, and Shay and Alma were her friends, they loved her, and they would always come to her birthday parties, just like they had since preschool. I took Dana back to bed, tucked her in and sat next to her, holding her hand until she fell asleep, and then Avishay woke up and said that he had just remembered he hadn't finished his math homework.

I told him that whatever he didn't do today he could do tomorrow, and he started arguing with me, groaning that the "teacher will kill me." I told him that Anat was lovely, that there was no way she would kill him for not finishing his homework, that tomorrow and the next day he would remind himself in his planner not to forget, and then he would only have to remember to look in the planner. I sent him back to bed and got into my own. Five minutes hadn't passed before I heard shouts of *"Ima, Ima,* water!" coming from Gali. I touched Yair's leg, but he was fast asleep, and I couldn't bring myself to wake him, so I got up again and gave Gali some water. Afterward, I went to the living room, to Yairi's desk, and checked my email. I responded to some messages, stared at Facebook for a while in search of some interesting news, and finding none except the same complaints by the same people, more pictures, the same "life is wonderful" display that made as much of an impression on me as a toothpaste commercial. I tried to go back to sleep, but sleep refused me, and so I lay down next to a man I wasn't sure I knew any longer, waiting for the sun to rise.

Chapter Twenty-Two: ITZHAK, NOVEMBER 1941

RUSSIA, ASTRAKHAN

When we got off the train again, we looked around us—it was late at night, and the platform was almost empty. Father said that we should spend the night there and come morning check on how to get to the Volga River, from where, according to his and Grandpa Eli's plan, we could sail toward Astrakhan to a better life. I was hungry and tired, but nobody was waiting to hand out bread. I snuggled into my own body, then leaned on my mother and stared at the bright sky blanketed by stars. Despite the hunger, hardship, and the fact that we were sleeping on a train platform, I was reminded of a sentence Father repeated over and over again: "As long as we are together, we are happy and whole. Don't forget it for a moment." I looked at my father's face and knew that I could trust him, and everything would be okay. The next day we headed for the Volga, which was near the train station. Before setting out, we stood clutching our ration slips for our daily serving of bread. We were so hungry that within two minutes, not a crumb remained. I noticed frustration spreading across Father's face. Forcing a smile, he said to me, "Ichu, we'll reach Astrakhan soon, and you'll see, it's going to be so beautiful, and we won't be hungry any longer. I'll find work, and everything will be okay." When Father spoke, I was so sure of the truth in his words that I said to him, "I know, Father, you don't need to explain things to me anymore, I'm almost nine."

In hindsight, I can look back at that hungry child clad in rags, whose young soul recognized the austere patience demanded of him, and I am reminded of the long years in which I didn't allow myself to acknowledge my hunger, not even for a second, in order to suppress my impatience and irritability. Childhood hunger exacts a steep mental toll over the course of one's life. It is not something you can fully grasp without experiencing yourself.

When we reached the Volga riverbank, we boarded a cargo ship, which had some people already on it, and set sail. I don't remember how long we sailed, but I do remember that numerous cities passed before my eyes, as well as children waving to me from the shore, and large groups of people, who appeared to be homeless, squatting at the edge of the river. From time to time, the ship stopped to unload cargo and reload some more. Father and Shimon assisted the ship captain, which allowed us to sail for free. At the first stop, Mother got off to exchange some ration slips for bread, while I opted to stay with Grandpa Eli to watch over our spot and our few belongings.

Eventually, we reached Astrakhan. I had imagined all the rich delicacies I'd gobble up and the beautiful house we'd live in, but while the city seemed pleasant, it also appeared neglected. It turned out we weren't the only ravenous guests who had arrived; an enormous number of immigrants affected by the war had fled to Astrakhan. Our fight for survival was far from over. We had come to an unfamiliar place, not knowing what the rules were—where we could go for a bit of bread, or what our living and work arrangements would be.

Chapter Twenty-Three: ICHU, NOVEMBER 1941

ASTRAKHAN

"Father found work! Father found work!" That's what I heard from Mother, who was speaking to Shifra, who told Sima right afterward and didn't get a chance to tell Shimon before I ran over to him and spilled the beans. Shimon had been running around all day looking for work and came up dry. While Shifra stood in the bread line, Sima went with Mother to look for a reasonable place to spend the night.

Shimon looked at me, shrugged and said, "Great! Now maybe we'll finally eat something besides a stinky piece of bread." I stared at him, and he stared back at me, and for a moment, I thought he might hug me, but the moment passed, and he didn't hug me, nor did I jump into his arms. We went to Mother and asked if she needed any help. Mother looked at us and finally, after a long time, I saw a smile break out on her face. "Come, my darlings," she said. "I found us a place to stay for a night or two, with some lovely people who agreed to host us. Can you give me a hand?" We picked up our few belongings and followed her.

The apartment was tiny, and inside were a man, a woman, and a little girl. The woman said to us, "Please, please, come in." We went in and Mother began to arrange a small area for us to sleep. I tried to be nice to the little girl and asked her if she wanted to play. Saying that she did, she thrust a fabric doll toward me. Shimon looked at me, holding back his laughter, and I said to her, "I'll hide your doll, and you can look for it. Then we'll switch. How does that sound?" The little girl nodded. I hid the doll in between the mattresses, and she searched high and low. After a while, I began to signal "hot" when she was getting closer, "cold" when she was getting farther away, and that's how the game went. She finally found the doll, hugged it to her chest tightly, and refused to play another round. Mother shot me a look that said *forget about it*, and in Polish said to me, "Let it be, I think that doll is her entire world." I went over to Grandpa Eli, who was murmuring his evening prayer. I sat next to him quietly, knowing not to disturb him, and then Father came in, breathless, and told us that he'd sailed to the other side of the river, hearing about some possible work, and how the business owner had told him he would only be able to pay in a bit of bread and a potato here and there—terms that he had immediately agreed to. "At least we'll have a little more food," Father said and looked apologetically at Mother, who appeared at a loss. She had hoped that we would lead a simpler life in Astrakhan, but so far, we had no stable living arrangement, and even working might not improve our circumstances by much.

The apartment was all right, but there were nights when mean people slept with us, like one family that hit their kids no matter what they did or didn't do, and we couldn't do anything about it since we didn't want to be kicked out. We were quite a lot of people, so nobody complained as long as we managed to find a place to rest our heads.

Playing with the little girl wasn't the same as playing with

Tzipke. Tzipke had been a true friend, and this girl always looked sad. In some places, people were nice, and their kids even nicer, so we got along well and played together, and when we needed to leave, I had already come to terms with the fact that I'd never see them again, not even on the street, and although that was a very sad thought, Mother and Father always told me that the most important thing was that our family was together, and every time I felt a twinge of sadness or loneliness, I remembered that Tzipke was counting on me to keep the coin safe until we met again.

I knew that whatever happened, the war would soon be over, and we would be able to return to our village, and everything would go back to how it had been before, other than the fact that Tzipke and I would be older and more mature; but the truth was, I never met another girl as pretty and as happy as she had been and who liked to get into the same mischief as me. One must focus on what's in front of him, not on the irretrievable past. I knew that I didn't have any reason to complain, I was one of the lucky ones, and that is the attitude I tried to preserve for the rest of my life—to be satisfied with what I had, to be thankful, and to always hope for the best.

Chapter Twenty-Four: MAYA, 2019

TEL AVIV

When morning finally arrived, breakfast was already on the table, and the lunch boxes packed up. Smiling, Yairi said that everything had its perks, including the fact that I hadn't slept a wink. On the way out, he left me dumbstruck as he kissed my forehead and told me to go back to bed and get a bit of shut eye. I almost muttered some nonsense about having a lot to do, but instead I just gave him a dazed smile, kissed each of the children, and closed the door behind them as they filed out with their father.

I stood there for a minute, leaning against the door, thoughts flooding my brain. Was my husband having an affair? Or had I let anxiety lay waste to my sanity and reason? And if he was having an affair, who was the woman who had won him over, and why? What did she have that I didn't, and where had our love gone, for God's sake? I went back to bed, cuddled into my blanket, and sunk into a deep, dreamless sleep. When I snapped awake, it was already noon. I jumped out of bed, ran a toothbrush over my teeth, and rushed outside. I was late to pick up the kids. On the way home, we stopped at a pizzeria. "Pizza for lunch!" I declared, and we all rejoiced.

When we got back home, I plopped the kids in front of the

TV for a pizza party while I went to my desk and stared at the computer screen. I called Itzhak's cellphone, and his caretaker picked up, saying something about a hospitalization and complications from a digestive blockage. I called Yair and asked if he could come home early so that I could visit Itzhak. He replied impatiently, saying that while he understood, I needed to understand that "Itzhak has a family, which you are not a part of, Maya. I'm working, and I can't just leave in the middle of the day because someone you work for doesn't feel well." I ended the call, feeling more upset than before.

Itzhak was like family to me. Maybe I was just looking for an emotional escape to flee from my own family? The thought crossed my mind as I wondered why I felt so connected to Itzhak. I didn't typically feel this attached to survivors whose stories I documented, but something about this man was different. His warmth, unwavering optimism, and verve for life moved me. He was in the hospital, and I just wanted to see him and make sure he was okay. I called my friend Racheli, who immediately suggested that I bring Avishay and Dana to their house, and she would pick up Gali in the evening. I thanked her, gathered a few of the kids' things, grabbed my bag, and left the house.

On the way to the hospital, I thought about the therapist I wanted to find and recalled that Racheli had once mentioned someone she'd gone to during a difficult period of her life. I called her again and asked if she still recommended her, and she said yes, adding that up until a year ago, she had seen Anat on and off but lately hadn't felt the need to do so, but "she's really excellent, and I trust her wholeheartedly."

"Maya, is everything okay?" she asked.

I replied that it was a "long story, not for right now, when the kids were around, but if you have time, we can meet for a coffee, and I'll tell you what's going on." Racheli gave me Anat's phone number, and we planned to meet the next morning at the neighborhood cafe.

After the call, I felt a little less alone. I had Racheli in my life, and Dalit and Keren, too, whom I hadn't seen in ages, but I definitely wasn't alone. I had good people on whom I could depend. I called Anat and left her a message, praying that she would get back to me quickly.

Night had already fallen when I got to the hospital. I found Itzhak lying in a hospital bed wearing striped pajamas, looking ten pounds thinner than before. He was sleeping, and his caretaker snoozed in a chair nearby.

"Itzhak's back where he started," I couldn't help thinking. But I banished the thought from my mind and sat down beside him. Not all Holocaust survivors had been imprisoned in concentration camps; people like Itzhak's family and many others experienced the pain of expulsion, displacement, hunger, death, and freezing temperatures—and they, too, were survivors, despite never having worn striped pajamas.

Itzhak was in a deep sleep, an IV tube stuck up his nostril, and he seemed weak. His caretaker whispered to me, "I've been here since the early morning. Can I leave you with him for a little bit? His son is coming soon." I texted Yairi, asking him to pick up the kids and bring them home by eight at the latest. "Racheli will give them dinner. I won't be back in time to put them to bed," I wrote, adding, "I'm in Jerusalem, in the hospital with Itzhak."

He responded curtly, saying that he understood that everything had worked out just like I'd wanted, and a bitterness swept over me, as if I'd been caught red-handed for some wrongdoing that I would later be punished for. Tonight, he would take care of the children while I took care of Itzhak; if he woke up and wanted to talk about his past, I'd write it all down, and if he didn't, I'd just sit by his side. If I saw that he was feeling a bit better, maybe I'd tell him about my discovery. Whatever happened, I would sit there until somebody came to take my place.

An hour later he woke up, looked over at me and smiled. Taking his hand out from under the blanket, he wrapped it around my wrist, his kind eyes shining.

"How do you feel?" I asked.

"I think maybe a bit better. What brings you here?"

I told him I'd called, only to hear that he'd been hospitalized. He looked at me quizzically and asked, "And what about your children?"

"They have a dad, too," I answered with a smile, but he seemed too tired to smile back. "I'm glad you're feeling a bit better," I added, trying to return the subject to him.

Itzhak nodded and said, "You know what's funny? During the war, I was so hungry all the time, there was nothing to eat, and now when I can have as much food as I want, I can't even swallow it. There's no justice in this world." He burst out laughing, and I joined in, but with a heavy heart.

We sat there for a few minutes, and then I said, "Are you ready to hear some good news?"

"I'm always ready for good news," Itzhak said and mustered a particularly mischievous smile. "So, tell me, did I finally win the lottery?"

"My news is even better than winning the lottery. I found Tzipke, or, to be precise, Tzipke found me," I said proudly.

Itzhak lifted his eyes in wonder. "My Tzipke? Are you sure it's my Tzipke?"

"Yes, I'm sure it's your Tzipke, but now her last name is Shmuelovitch not Voronski. It's a shame I didn't take a picture of her," I said. "I wasn't thinking straight."

Itzhak was silent and then asked, "Where did you even find her? Where does she live? Isn't she in America? When we sailed to Palestine she sailed to America, and I thought I'd never hear from her again." His mouth quivered and beads of sweat began to drip from his temples. "How is she?"

I replied that she was an impressive woman, that she looked and felt great, and didn't live in America, but in Tel Aviv, and that she had expressed interest in seeing him, if, of course, the feeling was mutual. Itzhak immediately replied, "Of course, of course, I would very much like to see her. The last time was when I was maybe sixteen or seventeen, and she was a year younger than me."

"It's really exciting to think that you haven't met since you were teenagers," I said, and he replied, "Yes, it really is. You were right, that was some great news. I thought the next time I would see her would be in the World to Come." Itzhak stopped to steady his breath. "A man can try to do a million things in his lifetime, but life will always have other plans for him. That is one thing I learned a long time ago." He waved his hand in the air as if to punctuate his point. "The fact that her family immigrated to America and ours came to Israel is a long story, which I will tell you one day. For now, I'll just tell you that my mother was adamant about not going anywhere if it meant being separated from any of her children, and Shimon, who had decided to join the Palmach at a time when many others were going to America, was in Palestine, so Palestine, it was. And voila," Itzhak concluded, tears clinging to his lashes. "You're telling me you found Tzipke…what a miracle…I can't believe this is happening."

When I saw his face, I understood the meaning of true love—the kind that could make one's eyes light up like shining stars, no matter how many years had passed, how many worlds and continents had been traversed. I was happy for him. I called Yairi to ask if he had finished work, but the truth was I just wanted to hear his voice. To my surprise, he said he was about to head out, and even asked how Itzhak was doing. Toward the end of the conversation, I said, "Thank you for leaving work on time to pick up the kids. I love you." Yairi responded, "I love you, too," and I hoped it was true. Turning back to Itzhak, I said, "If you'd like, when you're discharged from the hospital, I'll bring her to visit you."

"Of course," he said. "But tell me a bit more about how she is doing." I told him all that I knew, which wasn't much, and suggested that when they met, she continue telling her story where I left off. In the meantime, he needed to collect his strength and recover. I waited for Itzhak's son to arrive, and then we said goodbye, and I went back home, praying that it wasn't too late for us to make things right.

Chapter Twenty-Five: ITZHAK, FEBRUARY 1942

ASTRAKHAN

The days in Astrakhan passed slowly, with our main concern being what we would put into our empty stomachs. We were all very thin, and the adults had it worse than the kids. Every now and then, one of them got sick, Grandma or Grandpa, and Mother became anxious since there was no medical treatment to speak of. We were lucky that they eventually recovered, despite their ongoing physical weakness. We spent our nights in various places. The Russians made sure that each family had a roof over their heads, even in the private homes of families who received extra ration slips in exchange for hosting us. It was wartime, a time of scarcity, everybody was in crisis, not only us, although we were at the bottom of the pyramid—Jews, immigrants, refugees—lacking fluency in the local language, homeless, dressed in rags. At a certain point, we lived in a single room, but at least we didn't have to wander the streets, and when Father came home at night, he would always bring a serving of bread that was larger than what we'd been used to, once in a while, a few potatoes, and from time to time, some fat branches to add to the fire.

Then came the grueling Russian winter. Heavy snowfall was frequent, and the lakes froze over. The cold was so harsh that we could barely go outside. Early in the morning, when darkness still blanketed the air, Father woke up, got dressed quietly, and left for work. He travelled to the opposite side of the frozen river by tiptoeing on the ice, praying each time anew that it wouldn't crack under his feet, that he had stepped where the ice was thick enough to hold his weight. Father learned the river's ins and outs until he knew exactly where to put his feet. He managed to convince the peasant he worked for to provide work for another young man from our village whose family was going hungry. The young man began accompanying my father, and the two of them left every morning, returning every evening, tired and frozen, with the bit of food they'd received from the peasant.

Father instructed the young man, whose name was Lieb, on how to cross the river. He told him how and where to walk, and Lieb listened carefully, but one day, while in a rush, he didn't look where he was treading, and the ice cracked underneath him. With a shrill scream, Lieb fell into the raging river. Father, who was a very handy man, found a displaced tree trunk nearby and tossed it toward him, howling to the sky "Please, please, God of Israel, please save us." Lieb kept screaming, and it seemed as though the river was about to suck him into its depths. Lying flat on the ice, my father told Lieb not to let go of the tree trunk, and with great difficulty managed to pull him out and rescue him from certain death. Father wrapped Lieb in his coat, and the two of them shuffled, shivering and silent, to the opposite side of the river. Exhausted, they made it to the cabin, where they fell onto the floor. Mother, seeing how pale the two of them were, frantically ran to fetch them a cup of hot tea. She helped them remove their clothes and change into something dry, and then they sat near the fireplace that we had burning in the cabin. After regaining their strength, they told us what had happened, and from that day on, we spent every day in fear, praying that Father would return home safely from his work on the other side of the river.

In the meantime, we received a letter from Gail, my beloved aunt, who told us that her husband had passed away from his illness. We couldn't do anything to help her, and there was no way to bring her to where we were. The Russians had stopped the free movement of refugees as the war quickly made its way toward Astrakhan. They resettled many of them, including us, since we were considered "residents of unreliable loyalty," to another town, far away from the explosive noises. By doing so, they saved our lives. We took our few belongings everywhere we went and waited for ration slips, which we sometimes didn't receive for a few days. I don't know how we survived it all. I remember that I was constantly worrying—a child who was all grown up, trying to protect his family from harm and keep them together.

Chapter Twenty-Six: ICHU, FEBRUARY 1942

ASTRAKHAN

After two days of not eating, everybody received a serving of bread. I was so hungry I wanted to swallow it whole, but Grandma stopped me, reminding me that first we had to say the *HaMotzi* blessing, that the bread wasn't to blame for my hunger, and that I should nibble it gently. Then she added, "It's not healthy to eat so quickly." She almost ruined my appetite, but I was too hungry not to attack that bread with all my might. Glancing over at Mother, I saw that she was doing exactly what Grandma had ordered.

First, she said the blessing, then started in on her nibbling, instead of tearing it apart like a chicken leg. I said the blessing, bit down on the tasteless dry bread and didn't dare complain to Mother that I was still hungry because I knew she would give me whatever remained in her hands. Curling up into a ball, I waited in vain for a feeling of satisfaction to settle into my stomach. "At least something went in there," I thought. Grandma examined me and stroked my head. The corners of her lips turned up into a smile, and I couldn't help but copy her since her smile always made me feel warm inside. She said, "So, do you feel a bit better? At least you ate slowly, now you can imagine that you partook of a feast, and you'll see how full you feel." I smiled at her, thinking that old peoples' brains worked differently than mine, but what harm was there in pretending? I imagined us all gathered around the Sabbath table, full of fresh challahs and Mother's beloved cholent, and I wiped the tears from my eyes, because letting them flow would only make me feel worse and make my nagging hunger even harder to bear.

After the "bread feast," I asked Shimon if he wanted to play catch outside, but Mother said it was too cold, and that we should all stay together for her to tell us a funny story that happened to her when she was a little girl, and Grandma said that was a wonderful idea. We sat huddled together, sharing our body heat, and I was happy that at least the booms of cannons and fired shots that had been ricocheting around Astrakhan over the past few days had ceased. That night, and for the next few days, I hardly left the room we slept in—my coat wasn't warm enough to shield me from the cold, and the truth was it was already small on me, but I had nothing else to wear. There was no one I could complain to about my shrimpy, worn clothing, or my empty stomach—after all, we were all in the same boat together—so instead, I focused on counting how many hours of daylight there were and how many of night, and then I guessed when the sun would rise and set the next day, even though there were no clocks around to keep track of time.

Chapter Twenty-Seven: MAYA, 2019

TEL AVIV

On Saturday, Yairi's parents, my parents, and all our siblings came to Yairi's fortieth birthday party. While I whipped up some quiches and salads and baked his favorite chocolate cake, slathering it with frosting, the kids busied themselves making colorful cards, which I framed alongside pictures of their sweet faces. In the morning, I woke up early to close the bedroom door, so that Yairi could sleep in as long as he pleased. When he finally rose, I came into the bedroom, planted a kiss on his lips, and sang happy birthday as the kids jumped into his arms, which were open wide, lovingly ready to receive them.

I tried to push my negative thoughts to the back of my mind. Today I would think positive ones, if only for a day. Tomorrow we would have a talk, I decided. I couldn't live with all this doubt. The kids ran off to bring him the presents they'd made. Yairi promised to take the pictures with him to his office and put them on the wall, "so you'll be with me all day long, and every time I miss you, I'll just look at what you made me." Dana whispered to me, "Ima, I think we nailed this gift," and Avishay looked pleased, while Galush climbed onto Yairi's shoulders and told him that today was his day, that soon we would be singing him tons more birthday songs, and then she asked, "Ima, where's

Aba's crown? At school, whoever is celebrating their birthday always gets a crown. Where's *Aba's* crown?" We explained that Aba was already a big boy who didn't need a crown on his head to feel like a king, and besides, Yairi said, "*Ima* always makes me feel like a king."

Beaming, Yairi thanked me for my efforts, gave me a light hug, and said he had to call Moti about something important at work, since Moti would soon be asleep, and then it would be too late. I took the kids and left the room, falling back into my feeling of distress.

When the rest of the family arrived, Yairi reappeared with a wide smile across his face. I ignored the fact that he had been on the phone for more than an hour while I finished the party preparations. After everybody had gone home, Yairi said, "Thank you, Maya, I couldn't have asked for a better birthday," and I smiled and said that he deserved such a celebration every year. Then I opened my arms, and although he didn't pull back, I didn't feel any show of emotion.

He called out, "Gali, time for a shower, *Aba* will read you two bedtime stories tonight," and Gali shrieked with joy, while he told Avishay that he would come check his homework after he finished reading to Gali, and Avishay gave me a horrified look, as if to say, "Save me, *Ima*!" I said, "Dana, when you finish your shower, I'll brush out your hair, so that you won't have any knots." I told Avishay to shower in my bathroom, and to Yairi I said, "Let him be, it's late already."

Yairi replied, "Instead of making sure he does the minimum required of him, you're giving him brownie points for no reason." Avishay, frozen in place, looked at me, and I waved my hand as if to say that he should carry on with what I'd told him to do.

Then I turned to Yairi and said, "I don't understand what's gotten into you lately, but whatever it is, don't take it out on us." I saw that he wanted to respond, but I marched over to brush Dana's hair, and the evening ended in a huff and stalemate, despite the pleasant day we'd had together with our families. I was sure that my husband was going through something, and my attempts to raise the issue were rebuffed again and again, with him saying "everything is fine" and "you're the one who needs to relax."

Chapter Twenty-Eight: ITZHAK, MARCH 1942

ASTRAKHAN

One day, a man came to the refugee meeting point and asked if there was a shoemaker available. My father stood up and said that he was a shoemaker. We wondered what would be in store for him when the Russians found out that he wasn't. It was impossible to predict their reactions. Sometimes people disappeared for doing silly things, like saying something out of turn, or being suspected of lying or betrayal. People were taken from their houses, sometimes dragged right out of bed, never to return.

Father went with the Russian man, who took him to a workshop, and on his first day, he was given some minor jobs, such as adding a missing nail or fixing faulty threading. He made it through his first workday and returned home safely. We all jumped on him, hugging him tightly and pummeling him with questions. Father said he was tired, but besides that, everything had gone well. If we let him rest for a bit, he would tell us everything, one detail at a time.

After eating his daily portion of bread, Father told us how the Russian man had taken him to a small factory where they fixed old pairs of shoes. When he arrived, the factory owner had already finished his shift, leaving behind a few small repairs he hadn't gotten to. Father took over, and nobody noticed that he wasn't a professional. "But what will I do tomorrow?" he asked. "How will I hide the fact that I have no idea what I'm doing?" To this, Uncle Mordechai, Mother's brother, said, "Don't worry, tomorrow is a new day, and everything will be okay." Uncle Mordechai, it turned out, had learned the shoemaking trade for a time, as a young man. He promised to accompany Father and help him, and that's what he did. Uncle Mordechai and Father woke up bright and early and headed to the factory, where an additional piece of bread was waiting for Uncle Mordechai, and soon, the pair became great experts in shoe repair. Our daily portion of bread steadily grew, and we began to think we might like to stay in the town for a bit longer, but the echoes of cannons were approaching again, and it seemed as though the Germans were making their way deeper into Russia. Soon enough, the Russians told us to pack up and take the next train to a new destination.

Chapter Twenty-Nine: ICHU, MAY 1942

LEAVING ASTRAKHAN

We were on the train again. This time, I didn't sit next to Mother, but next to Grandma and Grandpa. Grandma began telling me a story about our synagogue in Tarnobrzeg, but explosions from outside shook the train car and made me shake like a leaf. I usually didn't mind train rides and liked the idea of going somewhere new. The weather had warmed up a little, and besides the stuffiness on board, everything was fine, until the bombing started. The Germans seemed to be blowing up the entire area, and everybody in the train car was praying. To stop myself from bursting into tears, I gripped the hidden coin in my pocket. It gave me strength and reminded me of Tzipke, which reminded me that this war had been going on for too long, and who knew when we might ever see each other again. For the first time, I began to doubt it would ever even happen. I could only hope that one day we would really reunite and pick up from where we left off. Mother sat next to me, hugged me tightly, and said, "Ichu, it really is a scary noise, but God is with us, and nothing will happen to us, I promise." When Mother makes a promise, she never breaks it, so I calmed down, and after a while, we had left the war zone behind and been saved once more. Mother had kept her promise!

The train kept chugging on to where, I didn't know. It was crowded, and Grandma didn't feel well. Suddenly, there was a lot of commotion in the car, but this time Mother didn't hug me, she hugged Grandma, while sobbing and rocking back and forth. Grandma whispered something in Mother's ear, and then her head fell back, and she became motionless. Grandpa and Mother and Father and Aunt Malka and Uncle Mordechai waved their hands desperately in the air and prayed. I asked Shifra what happened to Grandma, and she said that Grandma wouldn't be with us for the remainder of the journey. I had already seen death, when my aunt Hasya died, may her memory be a blessing, passed away while we were in the forest. Her soul left her, never to come back, even though I waited for a long time to see if she would come back and walk right through the door of our cabin, but she never did. I began to cry. I didn't want Grandma to leave. I looked at Shimon and saw him wipe a tear from his cheek. I loved Grandma Sara so much, her funny stories, the food she prepared when we had lived in Tarnobrzeg, the way she always soothed me when I was afraid or didn't feel well. She had kind eyes and a compassionate heart and knew how to find the good in everyone, even if it was buried deep inside. That's what my grandpa always said, over and over again.

I think that was the first time I truly understood death. It was a point of no return. Sometimes it came out of nowhere, and sometimes after a long disease, like what had happened to Aunt Gail's husband. The deceased go to the next world, that's what Grandpa told me, and that's where my kindhearted grandma had gone, to a world that was "all good, heavenly, and from there she will watch over us and everything will be okay." That's what

Mother said, too. After Grandma died, Mother wrapped her in a few rags that she had worn. We sat for a long time and cried together, even Shimon cried, and this time nobody laughed at the tears that gushed from my eyes like a waterfall, and at a certain point, I fell asleep, exhausted from my own sadness. When the train came to a halt, I woke up. While Father and Shimon collected Grandma's belongings, Mother kissed her. Then we sat back down and, since Grandma wasn't with us anymore, we hugged her raggedy coat that she had loved so much, and that had been with us since we'd left Tarnobrzeg. The men took Grandma into their arms and off the train; I don't even know where they took her, I only knew that I would never see my wonderful grandma again. It took a long time for them to come back, right before the train started moving. Mother kept crying until it was dark outside, and so did I, and Father stroked us both gently, promising that everything would be okay. Then it was quiet, and at some point, we all fell asleep.

Chapter Thirty: MAYA, 2019

TEL AVIV

The next morning, I took the kids to school then came back home to work on Ichu's story. Yairi had an extra early meeting "with the whole team from America, including the CEO." I called Ichu to ask how he was doing. In a cheerful voice, he replied that he felt much better. The blockage had been released, and he hoped to go home the next day if his vitals continued to be stable. "You don't know how happy you made me when you came to tell me about Tzipke," he said. "I didn't think I'd see her ever again, and you just came and gave me the best news I could have asked for. Maya, I have only one request," he added. "I want to see Tzipke, but it will be difficult for me to come to the Tel Aviv area. Do you think she would agree to come visit me?"

I said that we'd take it step by step, first allowing a little more time for his recovery, and then I would bring Tzipke to Jerusalem. "There's no way the two of you, a pair of young doves, won't see each other again," I said. "I've been excited for this meeting even before we planned it."

He asked, "Are you sure she'll be happy to see me? So many years have passed since the last time…," and I could only recall the twinkle in Tzipke's eyes when I told her about Ichu. I knew that the longer we waited, the less likely the reunion would occur, and I needed to do my best to make it happen. I told Ichu to try not to worry and promised that I would bring Tzipke straight to his door when the opportunity presented itself.

By the time I finished speaking to Ichu, I was already standing outside Anat's door. I had never been to therapy before, and I hadn't said a word to Yairi about it. Entering her home office, I was greeted by a large bookshelf, with books stacked clumsily on top of each other. Two plants flanked the shelf, and at the end of the room was a large, inviting sofa with an armchair on either side. Several pillows were scattered on the blue carpet.

Anat greeted me warmly, making me feel immediately at ease around this woman whom I had never met before. "How is Racheli?" Anat asked. "I haven't seen her in a while."

"She's fine. She sends her warm regards," I replied.

Anat asked me to tell her a bit about myself and what had brought me to her. She also asked if I was married, how many kids I had, and what my occupation was other than "being a mother." When she got to that question, I didn't know how to answer.

I told Anat that I documented life stories, and she asked if that was my life's work, if that's what I had wanted to do "when I grew up." She said I didn't have to answer that question now, or at all, and that, in general, I should feel comfortable answering or not, however I saw fit. My anxiety level dropped to zero, and within a few minutes, I felt as though I had made a close friend. After confiding about my big dream to be a best-selling author, I said, "Today I'm drowning in family matters, in my work, and I don't have much spare time for anything."

Anat responded by explaining that everything was a matter of priorities, and if I put my mind to something, it would happen. Then she asked me to talk about "the family environment in which you were raised," and that's how fifty minutes passed at the speed of light. I didn't even get to the real reason I had come, but I guess everything is related. Whatever happened there, I left with a gaping hole of four hundred shekels in my pocket and another appointment for the following week.

Anat's clinic wasn't far from Rabin Square. The weather was perfect, and I had some time to spare—priorities, after all. I could have gone home to work, but I decided to take a stroll instead. Happy for the opportunity, I took out the pair of headphones that had been lying neglected in my bag, and a moment later, Idan Raichel was crooning sweetly in my ears, brightening my day even more.

I had left Anat's office feeling that I needed to take a new approach to my problems. This resulted in me sending a message to Yairi telling him I'd arranged a babysitter, and that we were going out to dinner. "Cool, sounds good. I'll try to get home early," he replied. I told him that our reservation was in central Tel Aviv at eight o' clock, and we needed to leave early since it was Thursday, and traffic would be heavy. His response made me happy, and I made an appointment at the hair salon, calculating how much time I had left until I needed to go pick up the kids before heading to the salon. Then, with a new sense of purpose, I marched back to the car and drove home. On the way, I remembered that I had to call Tzipke and let her know about my conversation with Itzhak—and that he was in the hospital, but he couldn't wait to see her when he got out.

Chapter Thirty-One:
ITZHAK, NOVEMBER 1942

KOLKHOZ, SIBERIA

When we finally got off the train, after long weeks of travelling, we discovered that the Russians had left us in a ghost town. We had arrived in freezing Siberia in a small village that was situated near Kolkhoz, an agricultural commune from Stalin's time that had been built to increase production and settlement in the more remote regions of Russia and whose workers had to constantly prove their devotion to maximum efficiency. If the leaders found their work lacking, which happened on more than one occasion, they imprisoned the Kolkhozians, sending a message to the rest of the population as to what their fate would be if they neglected their work. When we were loaded off the train, the family was separated—Mother and Father were sent to work in Kolkhoz, far from the village, while Aunt Zelda, Grandpa, and the four children—I among them—remained within its borders. The Russians placed us in a widow's house. She lived with her two small daughters and was glum and quiet most of the time. Her husband had been killed in a battle against the Germans and was considered a great hero in the village, while her son had not been heard from since following his father into war.

We set ourselves up in a small room in the widow's house. What would we do in this remote village? When would we see our parents again?

We didn't know anything, and the days dragged on slowly. So did the war with no end in sight. The separation from our parents was difficult. We didn't see them very often and spent most of our time missing them. We missed their embraces, the family we once had, including those we had lost along the way, and yet the war kept raging. Father came around from time to time, with a few logs to replenish our fireplace and that of our host. Although he had been warned about going too deep into the forest where hungry wolves were waiting to devour him, our heroic father did just that, chopping down a few stumps and carrying them on his back through Siberia's horrifying cold terrain. The fact that we had a roof over our heads didn't stop us from freezing; without any heat, we regularly suffered from frostbite.

During the first days of our stay, we didn't get a word out of our host, but when Father came around with the logs and a bit of food he'd snuck from Kolkhoz, the widow was happy and thanked him. She shared that her son was on the front lines, and she hadn't heard from him for many days. Even the postman knew not to come bother her unless he had a letter from her son in hand, she said, sniffling through her tears. My sister Shifra walked over to the widow and placed her hand on her shoulder, but it only made her cry even more. A few weeks later, we heard shrieks of joy. We ran to see what had happened, and it turned out that a letter had finally arrived, and the son was still alive. He apologized for not finding an earlier opportunity to write to his mother and said he was doing fine. We all broke into a dance with the widow and her children, and it became a celebration. It was indeed wonderful to receive such heartwarming news during such a difficult time.

    We felt rejuvenated every time a letter arrived. The widow warmed up to us little by little, until eventually we felt like we were her adopted family. She shared her meager daily portion of food with us—some flakes of dough that had been cooked in milk and mixed with water. It was a treat. Warm food in the cold winter—a cure for both our hunger and our depleted spirits. The widow seemed to enjoy our stay, which made me feel a sense of security and solidarity with her and her daughters. They had experienced loss, anxiety, and death, just like us. I had never pictured myself living in a widow's home in Siberia. But the war went on and on, even though we prayed every day for it to be over.

Chapter Thirty-Two: ICHU, NOVEMBER 1942

SIBERIAN VILLAGE

I was actually quite happy when we arrived at the small Siberian village. It meant we could finally get off the train. We had been travelling for so many days that summer had already come to an end, snow began to fall, and I was cold and hungry. The train car was stinky, and the journey never-ending, so when we were told to get off, I jumped from my spot on the floor and rushed out as fast as I could. The Russians who were responsible for us Jews said that the strongest among us would be taken to work in Kolkhoz. I asked Mother what that was, and she explained it was a place where people worked and lived together. I made a face, reminded of all the times we had already had to live with other people, but this looked like it would be worse. It was really cold outside, but no one seemed to care. There was a lot of chaos, and suddenly, Mother and Father and Aunt Malka were taken off to work, while Grandpa and Aunt Zelda stayed with us. We said goodbye to our parents and aunt, and Zelda—who I loved the most because she is my funniest aunt—was loaded along with us onto a carriage that took us into town. There, we got off beside a small cottage, where a woman lived with her two young daughters, seven and nine years old.

As soon as I entered the house, I realized I would be cold, since she didn't seem to have any spare firewood, and I'd probably also continue to be hungry. The woman showed us to a small room, and we each set up a little corner for ourselves. We were lucky to have received a few ration slips, and Grandpa had made sure that Aunt Zelda waited in line so that we'd have some bread to eat. When we arrived at the house, we quietly settled in and waited for our host to crack a smile, which she never did. In the evenings, she and her daughters performed a funny ritual, where the girls kneeled before their beds, pressed their palms together and offered thanks for the food they had eaten and the water they had drunk. Sometimes it was for milk or bread or a stew that their mother had made, and sometimes they even offered thanks for the firewood they'd received from "the good man who brought it to us," meaning my father, who carried over branches from the forest whenever he came to visit us, and thanks to him, we all warmed up a bit. But the funniest was that when they finished being grateful for all of those things, they offered thanks for salt. What was so special about salty salt? That was beyond me.

Chapter Thirty-Three: MAYA, 2019

TEL AVIV

By the time evening came around, I had applied my make-up, gotten dressed, and every hair on my head sat elegantly in place. Yairi left me a message saying he would see me at the restaurant. "Our meeting got delayed a bit, wait for me, I'll get there on time," is what he wrote. Draping my red evening handbag over my shoulder, I said goodbye to the kids and to Noga, our babysitter, whom the kids loved as though she were their older sister. When I got to the city center, I parked near the restaurant with a few minutes to spare then strolled through Sarona Market, which had a different feel in the evening than during the day. Couples sat on benches, chatting pleasantly; soldiers clustered outside the restaurants, dragging their feet and joking around; a few young girls wearing long skirts flurried by. One of them, who was particularly slender and beautiful, exclaimed with a mix of astonishment and bitterness, "I can't believe she's getting married before us, who would've thought that the girl who said she'd never get married would actually be the first to do it!" Her friends laughed and agreed with her, and then they were out of earshot. When the clock struck eight, I went to the restaurant and the hostess showed me to my table.

The restaurant was packed with people, although it was a

midweek. I looked at the clock and saw that it was already eight-fifteen. The waiter approached me and asked if I wanted to order anything. I nodded and asked for a glass of champagne, which was placed in front of me in the blink of an eye. Glancing over at the front door, I waited for Yairi to enter, out of breath, and apologizing for his tardiness, but the door remained closed, and my cheeks burned at the thought of the people seated around me wondering what such a dressed-up woman was doing all alone in an expensive restaurant.

When an hour had passed and Yairi still hadn't arrived, I asked for the check, paid, and went back to my car. My eyes filled with tears, and I couldn't think of even one person with whom I wanted to share my pain. I felt an overwhelming emptiness, disappointment, and shame, and I wondered what I had done to give my husband the idea that he could treat me this way or, to be more precise, not acknowledge me at all. In the car, my tears collected into a storm, and the silence from my phone only exacerbated them.

Finally, my phone rang and in a flat, tired voice, Yairi said, "Maya, my meeting just finished, I hope you didn't wait for me." I hung up and drove home.

At home, I relieved the babysitter, who was surprised to see me returning on my own, and went upstairs. I first checked the children's rooms, tucked in their blankets, took the book off Avishay's bed, who, as was his custom, had fallen asleep with it open on his lap, and then went into the bedroom. At my small vanity table, I began removing my make-up when I heard the front door open. With heavy footsteps, Yairi shuffled up the stairs, made the same rounds I had just made, then approached the bedroom door I had locked. Standing in the hallway, he asked me to open the door.

"Maybe it was a mistake, opening up to you for so many years," I said through the wooden barrier that separated us.

"Maya, I'm really, really sorry. I don't have any excuse. Only an apology."

Behind the closed door, I said I knew he was having an affair, and that I "wasn't as stupid as he might think."

To my surprise, he didn't deny it, only asked me to open the door, and when I didn't respond, choking on my own tears, he begged. The door stayed closed, and I leaned against it, crying as I hadn't cried for many years, feeling entirely alone in the world. It wasn't a foreign feeling. I had known since I was a little girl that I was the only one who could find a solution to my own problems, that no one would lift me up if not myself. At a certain point, I heard him go downstairs. I stood up, got into bed, and covered my head with a pillow. Yairi slept in the living room that night and the next. We didn't exchange a single word.

The days passed, but they all looked the same. Yairi and I maintained a cold, functional relationship, and I was at a loss for what to do. I felt as though I had been left alone in the world, with only my children and Itzhak's story grounding me, reminding me that I still had a purpose in this world. I made sure to visit Itzhak as often as I could, to record more memories of his life. And I was lucky to have Racheli for support, and Anat, who had only recently entered my life. On Tuesday, exactly a week after the restaurant ordeal, I went to meet her. This time, we spoke about my childhood, past romantic partners, about the fact that when I met Yairi, I was sure I would "never find somebody who would truly love me, unconditionally, and now that he had broken my heart, I can't go back to trusting him ever again, and maybe I should just call quits on the whole thing." I spilled so many tears at that meeting, but one thing that Anat said did manage to get through to me.

"Maya, you are a people-pleaser, doing things that are good for others, while neglecting yourself. The world is a harsh place, and people like you, who give up on themselves, are liable to be abandoned by even their most beloved partners because they end up denying them their respect."

I left the meeting depleted of all my energy. I called Yairi and told him that I wanted to speak to him, that we couldn't go on like this, and he offered to meet me outside his office in half an hour. When I arrived, I told him to turn off his phone, knowing that if he left it on it would ring non-stop, and this time, he didn't argue with me. He turned off his phone and waited for me to speak.

Chapter Thirty-Four: ITZHAK, FEBRUARY 1943

SIBERIA

The days passed quickly. We got used to our routine in which we barely saw our parents, helped the widow around the house, and waited for the horrible winter to pass. My beloved aunt Zelda, who was staying with us, raised our spirits. Her bountiful joy was like nothing I had ever experienced, and her rolling laughter contagious. She had a unique sense of humor that surfaced during the most difficult moments. For instance, when we didn't have anything to eat, she suggested we melt some ice, dip it in salt, and drink it, as though we were sipping soup.

The funny faces she made took our minds off our hunger and sadness. She was so beautiful, and Grandpa Eli always said that it was "her biggest disadvantage for a beautiful woman always gets herself into trouble." Grandpa never explained why this was the case, and I didn't ask him back then, but when I think about it today, I assume he was talking about the long line of suitors who expressed interest in Aunt Zelda, which she elegantly ignored. Everyone who met her was stunned by her beauty.

Zelda fell ill that winter. At first, it was just a cold, and then a disturbing, heavy cough set in. Because we were far away from a clinic, Grandpa was quick to summon somebody who wasn't a doctor, but who "knew a thing or two about medicine." He examined her and said that she would "be all right," but Mother, when she came to visit, sensed that "something was off with Zelda." Mother went back to Kolkhoz, and the next day, despite the cold, she ran all the way back to the village, her intuition alerting her that Zelda was unwell. When she arrived out of breath and saw Zelda, her face fell. Zelda was burning up, and Mother didn't waste any time. Gathering up all the plants left over from the previous summer, which she had saved "for an emergency," she concocted a brew for breaking fevers. But the plants didn't do a thing. Zelda's fever refused to break. She ran back and begged the authorities in Kolkhoz to do something to save her sister. Soon a sympathetic crew arrived in the village by horse and carriage, onto which they lowered Zelda, covering her in blankets. Mother hopped on with them and off they sped to the hospital, a few hours' drive away.

In the hospital, they assessed Zelda's state and informed Mother that her sister had no chance of recovery. She had a severe lung infection, which they didn't have the means to treat. Poor Mother stayed with her beloved Zelda, taking care of her, easing her pain, and after three days, Aunt Zelda passed away, and Mother came back to us, shattered. Grandpa, who had always been a supreme source of optimism, withdrew into himself and his prayers. He was never the same. Losing Zelda, after losing his wife and his daughter Hasya in the forest, had broken him entirely. He isolated himself with his prayer books and was never again the Grandpa Eli I had known and loved.

We were also shaken up by Zelda's death. We loved her so

much. At first, in the days that followed, we didn't feel like doing anything at all. We couldn't stop crying. At a certain point, Mother said we had no choice, life must go on, that she would be all right and so would we, and so we returned to our established routine in our little room in the widow's house.

Chapter Thirty-Five: ICHU, MAY 1943

SIBERIA

The worst part of it all was that there was no one left to make me laugh after Zelda died. And although I had already understood that nobody who dies ever comes back to this world, there were days when I thought she might waltz right in and say that she had been sent to work in Kolkhoz for a few days and simply hadn't seen anybody who could pass along the message, and why were we all sitting there with sour, downtrodden faces? Then she'd say, "Here, while there's still snow, let's melt some and add salt so that our faces will be sour for a reason, and funny at the same time." On days when I had those thoughts, I would look at Grandpa Eli. He seemed to be waiting for her, too. He was so miserable. Losing Grandma and Zelda within the span of a few months was hard on all of us.

The cold days eventually released their grip and made way for spring to arrive, and after that, summer. Summer in Siberia was pretty and green. The ground was moist and grassy. There were no trees, only bushes. I think that trees didn't grow there because the brutal winter cold killed them all, just like it had killed those people who hadn't been able to get used to temperatures of minus forty-five degrees. Snowy mountains framed our village, which was close to the Baikal Lake, and if I hadn't known there was a war going on, I probably would have found the place perfect for a summer vacation. The lake became our summer fishing spot. We weren't always successful, despite the long hours we spent with our rods, which we fashioned from a branch and a metal hook. Once in a while, we'd catch a fish or two, which we'd eat gratefully and feel less hungry but not entirely satisfied. The hunger never really let up.

In the pleasant summer days, we played with the widow's children. Shifra brushed and braided their hair, aided by my sister Sima. The girls were very sweet and agreed to play hide and seek and catch with us, which happened to be my favorite games. Grandpa constantly warned us about the lake, which we had heard was the deepest lake in the world, but it didn't seem that way at all. I didn't know how to swim, and with the water being cold, we went in only up to our waists. Same with Shimon and my sisters. Grandpa kept an eye on us everywhere we went. After two of his daughters and his wife had died, he was terribly afraid of losing us as well. Whenever somebody got a slight cold, he immediately alerted Mother in Kolkhoz. We always listened to Grandpa, just as we had promised Father and Mother whenever they came to visit. I noticed that Father was always tired, and Mother terribly thin, to the point where I could see her bones sticking out from underneath her raggedy clothes.

When fall came around, it began to get cold again, and I kept thinking about how I couldn't stand to spend another winter there. We barely left the house, and it wasn't much warmer inside. One night, I heard Grandpa and Father speaking in hushed tones. Father was telling Grandpa he had heard that in Kazakhstan, things were a bit better, and that maybe we should ask the Russians for permission to go there. At first, I thought that's what we would do, pack up our things and go there, but then I wasn't so sure, because if we did, we would have to leave Aunt Zelda behind. We had left Grandma on the way to Siberia—I don't even know where—and Hasya in Camp 19, and it would be terribly sad to leave Zelda here forever.

Little kids need to play and eat well, that's what Mother said when she looked at us. She didn't know that I could hear her, but I could, and I wanted to tell her I wasn't a little kid anymore, and I understood the most important thing is that we're together. I know that together was all we had right then, but I also knew that the war would be over one day, and we would get to go home.

Chapter Thirty-Six: MAYA, 2019

TEL AVIV

"Listen," I said to Yair, "and listen closely. I'm not going to keep living like this. Not because I don't love you or because I don't care about you. It's precisely for those reasons that I refuse to do it. I choked the words through my tears. I looked at Yairi's kind eyes, at his formal work attire, and was glad I was wearing my flattering green dress, which never failed to perform its magic.

We were sitting in a café not far from his work. Someone could have come up to us at any point, so I did my best not to shed a single tear. I was sure I had done the right thing by meeting him near his office, and in public, because if we had spoken at home, our voices would have reached unreasonable volumes, and he would have stopped listening. He tried sneaking in some words as I was speaking, but I told him that I wasn't finished, and that he shouldn't interrupt me. As he sat back and waited for me to continue, I breathed deeply, then took out my sunglasses and slid them on.

"You don't share with me what you're going through. I know you have this 'Moti' character in your life, and I know that it's not your friend Moti, but a female 'Moti' you speak to late at night and dream about during the day." A sound emerged from the back of his throat, but I gave him a don't you dare look, and he didn't dare.

I continued. "I tried to give you time, thinking maybe it would help, but now I see that I made the wrong move for both of us, and especially for the children. We can't keep going on like this, Yairi, I can't do it anymore." Even though I was controlling my tears, he seemed unable to hold back his own, leading to strange looks, and me to look out the café window to see if the sky was still a beautiful blue, the sun still shining, the world still intact.

The long silence didn't disturb me; on the contrary, I felt as though a heavy weight had been lifted from my heart. Yairi's hand slithered across the table, but I moved mine away. "Can I say something?" he asked. I nodded.

"Listen, I'm sorry, Maya, truly sorry. I know I haven't been myself lately, and you've seen that. You always know that something's going on with me before I know it myself," he said, and a different expression came across his face. "Maya, I'm not trying to deny anything, but it's over. I ended it because I don't want anyone else but you, and I regret the whole thing. Nothing is worth your pain and tears. I don't know what else to say, Maya, but I'm sure of one thing: I don't want to lose you because I love you dearly, and I'm so sorry, so, so sorry. I was an idiot, maybe it was a mid-life crisis, maybe something else. But there's no excuse."

So, my instincts had been right—they hadn't misled me, I hadn't been imagining anything. A wave of relief washed over me, mixed with anger, desperation, and bottomless sorrow. I felt as though I was crumbling before the entire world, in this crowded café in an industrial area of Tel Aviv, in the middle of the day, and then I fell silent, trying to find my breath. Yairi sent his hand across the table again, and this time, I didn't resist his touch, letting my tears pour out; this time, I couldn't have cared less about the people around us. His confession had simultaneously broken and soothed my heavy heart. At least the secrets and lies were behind us now.

When I left the café, I called Racheli and told her that Yairi had confessed to having an affair, but also claimed that it was over, that he loved me and wanted us to stay together, that he was ready to do anything in order to mend our relationship, while I had told him that I didn't know what I wanted anymore and suggested that he go to a hotel for a few days so that we could both mull things over, stress-free, before deciding what to do next. Racheli called me a superhero, and said that she was "super, super proud of you."

I drove to the seaside, got out of the car, and sat on the beach, which was fairly empty. Staring out at the water was so calming, and as I breathed in the salty air, I reminded myself that I was worth something, just like Anat had said. I was important, my feelings were important, and I needed to consider my own welfare for once, even if it meant living separately from Yair. I still loved him, but our trust was broken, perhaps beyond repair.

Yair stayed at a hotel for the next few nights. He called a few times a day to ask how the kids and I were doing, and I replied politely, without asking after him even once. I told the kids that their father was on a business trip, and in the meantime, I met with Anat to discuss matters and spent a lot of time alone thinking about my own needs and desires. Anat asked me to examine "what your role was in creating these circumstances." Taking her assignment seriously, I began looking for answers.

I called my friend Rona, a family lawyer, and arranged a meeting in her office. When she asked, "Maya, is everything okay?" I replied, "Everything will be okay, but I'm a bit confused and don't know what to do. I think I just need to consult with somebody."

Rona said that she had my back, that I could call her anytime, but since my kids had afterschool programs, and I didn't want to disrupt our daily routine, I told her that it was nothing urgent. We planned to meet two days later.

When I arrived at her office, Rona had just finished a meeting with another couple, who left in a storm. Rona gave me a hug, said that I looked good and asked her secretary to prepare two cups of coffee.

Inside the lavishly decorated room, I sank into her comfortable red armchair, looked around me, and saw how Rona's radiant personality was reflected in the room's every detail. Since high school, where she'd been a star student, it was clear to me that Rona would have a successful career. She had known that she wanted to be a lawyer from a young age, and it was clear to me that she would put her heart and soul into whatever she set her mind to do. Filling Rona in on the past few months, I told her about my rough conversation with Yairi at the café and that he was living in a hotel.

Rona stood up from her seat, hugged me gently, and said, "Maya, despite all of the pain, and I know there's a lot of it right now, and despite all of the hardship you're going through, it's important for you to remember that not everybody has what you and Yairi have. Every marriage has its crises, its ups and downs, and cheating is really an awful thing that has the potential to destroy a lot of couples." She paused. "Just so you know, you're always welcome in my office as a friend, but typically couples come to me after having established that their love is really dead, and I don't think that's the case with you and Yairi. Am I mistaken? Please correct me if I am."

With tears in my eyes, I told her that it was possible the rupture between Yairi and me couldn't be mended because when trust is broken, it's almost impossible to return to the way things were. But that didn't answer her question about love.

Rona looked at me sternly and said, "Listen, I understand that you're in a moment of crisis, but I also think that in your case there's a good chance your wounds can heal. You're a strong couple and based on the fact that you avoided the love part of my question, I understand that there must be some left. A bit more communication won't hurt anybody. Would you like the name of a good couples' therapist?" In between sobs, I nodded.

On my way back home, I called Yairi. I told him that I had a contact for a couples' therapist and asked if he wanted to set up a meeting. He replied with an eager "yes."

The next few days, I spent at Yad Vashem, collecting more research on the paths taken by Polish Jews in Russia—the number of refugees from the area, their varied circumstances for leaving their homes, the disparate directions they ended up going, and other information about the war as it impacted central Russia. I thought about Itzhak's family, and how they had fled further inside the landmass whenever the war came too close because of the Russian mistrust of Jews as "a foreign population whose loyalty couldn't be trusted"—an attitude which ended up saving Itzhak's family.

Chapter Thirty-Seven:
ITZHAK, DECEMBER 1943

SIBERIA

After my aunt Zelda's death, there was no chance that our lives would go back to the way they had been. There was a feeling in the air that the war would soon end, but the loss of three of our family members had taken its toll. My grandpa was broken. He became immersed in his prayer books and in his own thoughts. It seemed as though he had lost all hope, which affected us, too. In the summer, rumors of European Jewry's terrible fate under the Nazi regime reached faraway Siberia. There were few Jewish families around us. Grandpa Eli joked with them, "How much for a few words of optimism? Just name your price." Even the pessimists among us couldn't have fathomed what fate lay in store for the Jews. Some refused to believe it, thinking that the rumors were simply fanciful stories fabricated by the Siberian villagers.

My sister Sima told us that one night she woke up and saw Grandpa Eli praying intently from his prayer book. Bent over the lantern propped up in a corner of the cold room, he was sitting as though he didn't even notice how freezing it was. She wondered whether she should say something, but he was so absorbed in his prayers that she decided not to disturb him. In the morning, Sima asked Grandpa why he chose to pray on these especially difficult, cold nights, without covering himself up. He replied that it was the least he could do for his family who he'd left behind: two of his sons, his daughter Gail, and their families, "and the rumors, the horrible rumors, somebody please prove them wrong." Sima recounted this story to me later, as I was struggling to make the connection between the optimistic man I once knew and this praying figure who foreshadowed only pain.

The year 1943, which was almost over at this point, had left us deeply scarred. The unbearable cold, the frightening snowstorms, and our constant state of malnutrition had battered each one of us. We were weak and defenseless. My parents were hard at work in Kolkhoz, and the rations they received in exchange were so meager, they, along with Grandpa, had begun brainstorming where to go next. My parents, Grandpa Eli, and the remaining Jewish families in Siberia—many of whom had also lost family members—decided to ask the Russian authorities for permission to leave the village and move to a more central location. Our request was granted. Packing our belongings once again, we headed for the southern city of Zhambyl.

Chapter Thirty-Eight: ICHU, DECEMBER 1943

EN ROUTE TO KAZAKHSTAN

On a day no different from any of Mother Russia's other harsh, cold winter days, we had stayed at home to keep warm, when suddenly Shimon tried to get up but instead fell forward onto the floor. Only a moment before, I had been telling him a story about a dog I'd petted earlier that day, and then he fell, sprawled out on the floor, and I was sure he was dead. I shouted, "Shimon, don't die, Shimon, don't die!" and Grandpa ran to open my brother's clenched jaw to allow oxygen to enter his body. We stood around him shouting, and the crazy neighbor ran to Kolkhoz and told Father that his son Shimon had died, adding that she'd seen it with her own eyes.

Telling the neighbor not to say a word to Mother, Father ran with all his might all the way from Kolkhoz to the village in the blistering cold, praying that there had been a mistake, that his beloved son Shimon was still alive. When he arrived and saw Shimon sitting there, surrounded by everybody else, he burst into tears. He hugged Shimon so tightly that it seemed as though he would run out of oxygen again, and they both cried. When I saw them crying, I hugged them, too, and couldn't help but cry with them. I didn't know what I would do if my brother Shimon died. He was my best friend in the entire world, and his presence gave me the strength to survive the war. It was a miracle, truly a miracle. While Grandpa sat in the corner and steadied his breath, Sima and Shifra calmed him down with their warm embraces; only Mother was missing, so Father returned to Kolkhoz to tell her what had happened.

After what happened to Shimon, Father started speaking differently to Grandpa and the others about this place we were living in, which we had originally thought wouldn't leave us so cold and hungry all the time. They were thinking about leaving the area where there were few, if any, doctors, but I didn't want to leave even though I was hungry and cold most of the time. We had already gotten used to the friendly widow and her daughters, had a roof over our heads, and even though Mother and Father didn't live with us, Grandpa did; our parents came to visit whenever they could, and whenever Father brought a sack of firewood, we were all content under the widow's low roof. But one day, Father stopped by and told us we were leaving, just like that, and the widow burst into tears, saying that she understood, and that she would be forever grateful for his good nature, and for his help getting her through the winter. We gathered up our belongings yet again, said goodbye to the widow and her children, who were really so nice. It had been so much fun to play with them, even games meant for boys. We went to the train station and got on the next train going south, to a new place, which I didn't know the first thing about.

Chapter Thirty-Nine: MAYA, 2019

TEL AVIV

On Thursday, we went to see our couples' therapist. Yairi told his side of what had happened over the past few months and apologized for breaking my trust. The therapist didn't pressure him into saying anything specific, so I asked him to start from the beginning—the very beginning. "I want to know everything, what happened and why. That is my wish, Yairi," is what I said. "It's very important to me. I need to understand and process in order to forgive. Right now, I'm very hurt, and it's difficult for me to see how we can move on."

The therapist said that while she understood that's what I wanted and how I felt, she said, "Yair's words, and when he chooses to speak them, are up to him. Maya, many couples go through what you're going through now, and things take time, so I'm asking for your patience. It's only our first meeting, and you're here not only to speak to each other, but also to get to know me. Besides, it's important that you both know that when someone has an affair during a marriage, it's almost always related to both partners and to poor communication. We'll work on that together—on communication and openness, in addition to building trust—in this safe space."

As the therapist spoke, Yair stared at her and then at me, and when she finished her speech, he turned to me and said that he wanted to share everything, but he wasn't sure how I would feel after it all surfaced. "I don't have anything more to lose," he said with tears in his eyes. I saw that his knee was shaking, and his cheeks were flushed; I even pitied him a bit, despite my anger, but then a horrible thought entered my heart: Let him suffer a little, question my love for him, our partnership, and our family, feel foreign in a world that was so familiar up until a few days ago.

Yair looked at me, and then at the therapist, and the words came pouring out of his mouth, trying to justify his actions, despite saying that he didn't blame me for anything, only hoped that one day I would be able to forgive him and move on. I listened to him speak, without offering a reply, but my heart was torn in two. I was ashamed, even humiliated, that my husband had chosen to pursue another woman besides me, had chosen to give somebody else his attention at the expense of his family. It was hard for me to let go of that maddening thought. When our time was up, we scheduled another meeting for the following week; outside the building, Yair asked if he could come see the kids on Saturday, and I said yes, but that I wouldn't be home.

Yair arrived on Saturday morning. Jumping on him, the kids asked where his bag was, and he said in the car and that he'd bring it later, since he might need to go back to work in the afternoon. Surprised, they asked, "What do you mean, on a weekend?" and he replied that it was still Friday night in America and meetings were still going on. They laughed, not quite understanding how time differences worked, which put Yair at ease, and Gali asked, "Aba, where are our presents?" Dana glanced at Gali knowingly and said, "*Aba* doesn't always have to bring presents when he comes back from a business trip, Gali." Yair looked at the kids and said, "I didn't have a single free second this time, but I promise that next time, I'll buy each one of you loads of presents, not just one." The kids shrieked with joy, Yairi spun Gali in the air, and Avishay said, "Aba, we're just happy you're here, we don't really care about the presents. We don't need anything else." Gazing at our children, I was so proud of them, and suddenly, I longed for those Saturdays we had spent together as a family. I missed our morning strolls, as well as those cozy days at home, and as I shifted my gaze to Yairi, I wondered whether he might be thinking exactly the same thing.

When I was about to leave for coffee with Racheli, he asked if we could speak when I got back, and I said yes. He asked the children, "Who wants to go to the park?" and they all jumped for joy. As I opened the door, I heard Gali ask, "Why isn't Ima coming with us?" I couldn't make out Yairi's response, but soon enough, I found my face uncontrollably wet with tears again.

After meeting Racheli, I headed to my parents' house. They were disappointed to see I'd come alone. Was I not enough? I didn't want to say anything that would end in an argument, in which they would probably accuse me of being "strange," something that happened whenever I said something they construed as a complaint. So, I didn't say anything, only that Yairi had decided to have a "Daddy Day" with the kids, and they didn't ask any more questions.

Sitting there, I looked at my parents, who had been together forever. He still served her coffee, and she thanked him and baked his favorite cookies, even though their relationship was far from perfect and despite my mother's rough personality and my dad's overly dovish outlook. At the end of the day, they were still together. Yairi and I, on the other hand, were ten years into a marriage full of love and friendship that had just taken a sharp turn. I was reminded of our most treasured moments together and wondered again if our relationship could ever return to what it once was. It was almost as if I had forgotten that beyond being a father, Yair was also a human being and my partner. I tried to think, perhaps for the first time, what my role had been in creating these circumstances—maybe my obsession with scheduling, my grab-and-go meals, which I often ate standing up, loads of stress, and endless exhaustion. "How did I not see this coming?" I asked myself for the millionth time, and suddenly, I knew the answer: It's not that I had stopped loving Yairi. I had just stopped seeing him. Maybe I hadn't noticed what he needed from me in order to feel loved? And what I needed from him?

I left my parents' house, my melancholy still gnawing at me, and drove to the sea to watch the sunset, breathing deeply in a way I hadn't in a long time. The sky was a bright red, the water still. I couldn't remember the last time I'd felt so calm and thought that maybe it was premature to give up on my marriage, that there was still a chance it could be salvaged.

When I got home, the kids had already bathed, Yairi was reading a book to Gali, Dana was lying in her bed, half-listening to his voice, and Avishay was reading his own book in bed. Yair's face lit up when I walked into the room, and I sat on the edge of Dana's bed and asked him to keep reading. After tucking everyone in, we wished the kids good night, and Yair offered to pour us both a glass of wine. We sat in our tiny garden, and immediately, conversation began to flow. We spoke about our feelings, hurt, betrayal, and disappointment. Yair told me about Ye'ela whom he had met on a business trip in Silicon Valley. They worked together for a few days, Ye'ela helping him promote a project he had tirelessly been working on, with the hope that someone in management would acknowledge his efforts. "She really believed in me, kept on giving me compliments. It felt good to be around her." Eventually, their relationship developed into "something more, in this totally unplanned way," he said, and I felt my heart convulsing inside my chest.

I still wasn't sure I could forgive this man who had once been so close to me. Yairi apologized again and suggested coming home, if I had any love left in my heart for him, because he was certain of his love for me. After thinking for a moment, I told him that he could come back on a few conditions: First, he would sleep in the living room until further notice—to this, he agreed immediately. Second, we would continue couples' therapy, which he had no problem with either. And thirdly, we would get a babysitter once a week for a few hours and go out just the two of us—where, wasn't important. Yairi smiled, and I gazed at him hoping that one day the storm would pass, and our love would win the devil's dance that had been contaminating our life.

Yairi drove to the hotel for his things, while I went upstairs to get ready for bed. When he returned, I heard him shuffling around in the living room, and I missed our intimacy even more. I slept more soundly that night than I had in a long time.

In the morning, I awoke to a steaming cup of coffee and a table full of giddy children, dressed and ready to leave the house.

"How did you do all of that without waking me up?" I asked Yairi. Avishay said, "*Aba* said we were on a mission to let you sleep in! It was a surprise!" Dana laughed and said, "We almost finished the mission, but then you woke up." Gali simply jumped in between my legs, asking if she could have some chocolate milk, and Yair replied that her chocolate milk was "almost ready, Gali, let your mother drink her coffee in peace."

Yairi and the kids said goodbye to me and Gali, and before they left, Yairi said that he would try to come home early that evening, maybe even in time for dinner, and the kids overheard him and were happy, and truthfully, so was I. On the way to Gali's preschool, I was fine not seeing Matan's hot dad, especially in the sweatpants I was wearing, which I chucked into the garbage as soon as I got home. Picking my new outfit carefully, I dressed as if I had an important meeting to get to, which I did—with myself. I was important.

Later in the day, I called Tzipke and asked if she wanted to arrange a trip to Jerusalem to visit Itzhak. "Now that he's feeling better, I feel like it's a good time," I said. Tzipke was delighted, so we made a date, "after the Shavuot holiday, exactly two weeks from today." As an active mother at Gali's preschool, I had volunteered to come help out at the Shavuot party.

Chapter Forty:
ICHU, DECEMBER 1943

RUSSIA, ON THE ROAD

We were on the train again for many hours—the snow outside the only unchanging part of the landscape. We approached and left behind numerous cities, the cold seeping through the walls of the train cars, and I was hungry, so hungry, all the time. Then, after a few weeks of riding with my stomach eating itself from the inside, Father fell ill, and I feared he would die. He was so weak, and Mother gave him her special boiled herb brew to sip, assuring me that he would get better. "He only needs to regain some of his strength, and everything will be okay." That's what she promised, but I didn't know if I could believe her anymore because it wasn't the first time she'd promised that everything would be okay, and then nothing was okay. But I didn't say anything. I just stayed quiet and held her hand, doing my best not to cry, not even once, even though I wanted to almost all the time. Then we arrived in the city that we'd been promised would provide us with a better life. Mother asked Shimon and Grandpa to help her get Father off the train, and from the train, they took him straight to the hospital, while the rest of us went to some crowded apartment, maybe fifteen people in one freezing room, and I was hungry again. We received more ration slips for bread, and my sister Shifra stood in line and brought a small piece for each of us, which I ate really slowly to trick my stomach into thinking it had actually received something substantial, and I missed my parents. I saw Mother very little, since she was spending most of the time in the hospital with Father, and when she came back, she fell asleep immediately, only to disappear again in the morning until the wee hours of the night. Father, I didn't see at all. I begged to go see him, but Shifra tried convincing me that "The hospital is no place for little kids," even though I was already almost eleven, but I didn't say a word because I knew her intentions were good, and she was trying to protect me.

I looked at Sima, who wasn't allowed to go see Father, either, and we both rolled our eyes like know-it-alls and begged Grandpa tell us a story from the Torah—so he told us about Jonah the Prophet. "Do you remember what was depicted on the ceiling of our synagogue in Tarnobrzeg?" And we said together, "Of course, Jonah the Prophet's whale." The memory was crystal clear in our minds, even though the village seemed lightyears away, the years we'd spent as nomads so long and painful, the end of the war nowhere in sight—but how could we forget such a thing?

It seemed as though the war made a point of following us wherever we went, which forced us to pack our bags again and wander off to a place even further from home. Maybe by the end of it, we'd reach the end of the world, and then I could only hope that the war wouldn't reach us there. Grandpa told us again the heroic story of Jonah's prophecy about Nineveh, explaining that Nineveh wasn't too different from the evil Germany, and the whale of the belly was like Russia watching over us, and that one day we would emerge from it and return home to our synagogue. Sima and I looked at one another and thought that maybe our wise Grandpa was right after all, that one day the war would be over, and we would go home, just like in the story.

Then one day, Mother brought Father home with her. He looked so weak, sick, and thin that it was frightening. His muscles had disappeared, his bones stuck out, and even though we were relieved he had returned to us, we were still afraid that he would die since it was so cold at home, even though winter was almost over, and the snow had begun to melt, and spring was budding slowly. We didn't say anything, only repeated what our nosy Russian neighbor had told us, "Kids, if you want your father to heal, pay a visit to the woman on the next street over. Knock on her door and tell her you need to make mashed potatoes for your sick father." Mother thought she'd come from outer space—who in their right mind would give us potatoes when their own kids were going hungry? But we begged Mother to let us at least try, and Mother saw that she had nothing to lose, and finally agreed, but told us to be as polite as possible, not to just barge into a stranger's house, and to return home immediately afterward, even empty-handed.

Sima and I promised, and off we marched. We knocked on the door quietly, but there was no answer, and then Sima said, "Ichu, I think that if we don't knock any louder, we won't get any mashed potatoes for Father, and I think we both know he's in pretty bad shape." We knocked a bit louder and waited, hearing slow footsteps, and then the door opened, and a slight, thin woman stood in front of us. She asked who we were and what we were doing at her door. We explained that our father was sick, and that the neighbor had told us mashed potatoes might make him feel better, adding that our mother didn't want us going into her house, but that we could tell she had a kind heart just by looking at her face. The woman smiled and said, "Wait here a minute," and she didn't even close the door, even though it was already evening and had become quite cold. We waited for a few minutes, and then she came back with some potatoes, and we wanted to jump for joy, but we stayed with our feet on the ground and thanked her politely, just like we'd promised Mother. Stuffing the potatoes in our pockets, we ran home, and Mother smiled at seeing us. "Sima and Ichu, bless your souls, you've done well." Later, she murmured, "I just hope it'll make him better." Mother cooked the potatoes and fed Father slowly. The next day he rose from his bed. His fever had broken, and he felt a little bit better.

Chapter Forty-One: ITZHAK, FEBRUARY 1944

ON THE ROAD

The journey south was long and exhausting but brimming with anticipation. Father, Mother, and Grandpa hoped that a semblance of our humanity could be restored in the big city, where we would no longer be in the center of conflict. Rumor reached our ears that steps were being made toward appeasement, but the overall situation was still trying, especially for the refugee population. When we got onto the last train toward Dajlimbrad, Kazakhstan, Father fell ill and was struck by a boiling hot fever. The anxiety that he might not survive the trip gnawed at us all, and when we reached the city, we immediately took Father to the hospital. He lay in the hospital for weeks, causing our spirits to waver from steadfast faith to despair. Mother remained by his side, tending to him, while we took to an abandoned, derelict room—Grandpa and four children, some of us already young adults, suffering from cold, anxiety, and unbearable hunger. Winter would soon be upon us, as unforgiving as ever. Frostbite permeated into our bones, even though we had gone south. Our greatest hope had culminated in bitter disappointment. I can't say I have any fond memories of Djalimbrad.

A Russian neighbor suggested collecting leftover coals to warm our room. She also let herself wonder out loud how we were going to survive this period. People were dying on the streets, mostly children, and the sight was devastating. We all went out to look for scraps of food and coal. The days turned to weeks, but Father's condition did not improve, and at a certain point, the doctors decided that his chances of recovery were slim and sent him "home." Father arrived at our small room, and we took care of him as best we could, with love and embraces, which lifted his spirits. Slowly, his condition did improve, a true miracle; like magic, he got better and came back to us. He began to look for work, doing whatever it took to bring us home a loaf of bread. Although we had gone south, the winter months were the most difficult we had experienced. The cold chilled our weakened bones. Even though Mother also accepted every odd job that was offered to her, we were hungry all the time.

After that horrible occasion when my brother Shimon fainted, we all tried to keep an eye out for him. But Shimon, who was already seventeen years old, decided he was healthy and strong, and he too went out to look for work. It was a difficult search. But one day, he informed us that he had seen "some kind of smoke screen rising toward the sky and merging with the clouds." His curiosity led him to the screen, which turned out to be the steam from a crowded factory. When he approached the factory and peeked inside, his eye caught a pair of impressive boots. He thought, "How lucky are the people who wear those boots and are spared even a single day of cold." And suddenly he heard, "Hey, kid, what are you doing here?" Turning toward the man, Shimon received a warm, welcoming smile that melted his heart. He answered the man, "I'm not a kid, I'm already seventeen," and the man laughed aloud and said, "You're seventeen?

Unbelievable. You are as thin as a little worm. But if you say you're seventeen, maybe you want to help us out here in the factory?"

"Yes, yes, I want to help, I want to work." The man invited him inside to make a pair of boots. A rank smell of leathers and glues summoned him forward. There were only a few laboring workers in the factory. "This is where we move along the leathers," the man, whose name was Yasha, explained. "And here is the sewing station, and here is where we straighten the soles before plastering them on." Shimon turned around, in awe of the factory's inner workings. Yasha led him to the sewing station and showed him the ins and outs of the job: sewing the leather and sole together and making sure that "everything was properly reinforced."

Shimon sat down at an unmanned station and began to work. Yasha quickly saw that Shimon was a hardworking, intelligent boy, and at the end of the day, he asked if he'd like to come back the next day. Shimon enthusiastically agreed, and Yasha declared the job his. The pay would be minimal, but he could eat lunch in the factory every day with the rest of the workers.

"You should know," the boss told him, "these boots are made with love for the heroes of our great Russian nation, who are fighting day and night, sacrificing themselves for our survival, to protect their people and our country." And Shimon replied, "It is a great honor to do this work, with great affection for our soldiers on the front." Yasha understood that a loyal worker had fallen into his hands. His reply was, "From now on, I will no longer call you a boy since you have proven yourself mature and responsible." And that's how it was.

Chapter Forty-Two: MAYA, 2019

TEL AVIV

Over the following days, Yairi came home early, and we even went back to eating dinner as a family. His night phone calls became less frequent, and when they did take place, Yairi made sure that I could eavesdrop if I so wished. He kept the study-playroom door open, even when the kids were asleep; they slept deeply, and his conversations didn't wake them up. Yairi wanted to demonstrate that his willingness to change was genuine. He was an open book and shared his feelings on just about everything.

I continued my sessions with Anat, discovering myself anew, as a person—not as daughter, a wife, or a mother—as myself, without any relation to those around me. Who was I, really? What interested me? What did I enjoy doing? What were my hobbies? My dreams? I had neglected these questions for years, focusing on those around me, forgetting myself, giving up on my relationship in the process.

One Tuesday, like every other Tuesday—as we had decided two weeks earlier, and a few days before I was to go with Tzipke to meet Itzhak in person—Yairi and I paid a visit to our marriage counselor and then went out to a restaurant. I thought the session had gone well, especially since I noticed how much Yairi truly wanted to right his wrongs from the bottom of his heart; he kept asking the therapist if she saw the potential for a true mending of our relationship. The therapist asked me my feelings on the matter, about the chance for true repair, and I replied that we were on the right track, that if both of us truly wanted it, then it would be possible; and I smiled at Yair, who squeezed my hand in return, brought it to his lips and kissed it tenderly. We stayed like that, hand in hand, all the way into the Tel Aviv evening awaiting us.

I was quiet most of the way to the restaurant. Out of nowhere, Yair said that the therapist had made him see things in a different light, and I deserved better than the way he had treated me. My breath caught in my throat. He moved his hand toward mine again, and whispered, "Maya, I'm so sorry. It wasn't okay, and it won't stay this way, I promise."

Although a few weeks had passed already, Yairi still slept in the living room after the children fell asleep and woke up before them. At dinner, I told Yairi that he could come sleep with me, and when we got home, we let the babysitter off the hook and went up to the bedroom holding each other tightly. I shed him of his clothes, and he shed mine. There we stood, ogling one another, until I approached him and led his hand to the places on my body that longed for his touch. I told him I had forgiven him, and I meant every word.

When the tension had cooled, we lay down together in a warm embrace. I asked if he still wanted to take that family vacation to the parks in Holland in August, and he replied that he wanted to very badly, that he missed spending quality time as a family. We started spending our evenings organizing the trip together, and I decided to put everything that had happened behind us, but I would retain the lessons I had learned in order to preserve the good parts of our relationship. I decided to live life to its fullest, to appreciate all that I had, and to keep working on our connection.

The next day there was a Shavuot party at Gali's preschool. Yairi couldn't get off work, so I invited my parents. Gali was thrilled when I told her, "Abba won't be able to come, but Saba and Safta will." I left the two older ones with their friends and arrived at the party early to help set up. And then, when we were almost ready for action, I heard a "hello" from the entryway. Lifting my gaze, I saw that Tzipi Shmuelovitch had arrived accompanied by Matan, Gali's best friend from preschool, and Lior, the hottest dad in class, who always made me feel as if I should have primped myself up a bit more. This time I was wearing a white dress that worked wonders on my curves; I was made up elegantly and welcomed the opportunity to give my all to that hottie flashing me his million-dollar smile.

I smiled back at him. Only when I took a good, long look at him did I finally connect the dots: Tzipke Shmuelovitch was Lior's mother and Matan's grandmother. How had I not realized this before? Lior was her spitting image, with those deep blue eyes, rounded chin, and high cheekbones. I approached them and extended my hand for a shake. My mother stepped toward Tzipke and offered her a hug. She barraged her with questions: "What was she doing here? How did she come? Who was that man she had arrived with?"

"Oh, I see the resemblance now, and which one is your grandchild?" From within this storm of questions, answers, and parents who had paraded into the preschool, I found myself speaking with Lior, blushing, brushing aside my stray hairs and straightening out my white dress. Luckily, the preschool teacher called out for the guests to sit down, and the festivities began.

I took out my camera and snapped shots of Gali dancing in the center of the circle with Ziva, the teacher. I was so proud of my sweet girl, and from time to time, I snuck a glance at Lior the hottie, who was sitting directly in front of me, and I saw that he, too, had pulled out his phone and was taking photos of Matan.

After the performance, the teacher gave a short speech, and then a committee representative was asked to thank all those involved. I volunteered to speak and praised those sweet children, reminding everyone that we were still collecting funds for the end-of-year party. Afterward, snacks were served, and I whispered to my mother that I needed to pick up the kids. Deep in conversation with Itzhak's Tzipke, she refused to leave, while my father stood next to her without uttering a peep as usual. I told him I was happy he had come, and he said, "I should be the one thanking you for inviting us to Gali's wonderful celebration." He so often hid in my mother's shadow, but from time-to-time, he uttered pearls of gratitude that washed a soaring wave of love over me.

I pretty much had to drag my mother out of the event when it ended. My father stood by her side and quietly suggested that it was time to go, but she ignored his remarks as usual. Only when I ordered, "Out. Now!" were we able to nudge her to the door and toward the car.

We picked up the kids and drove home, where Yairi was waiting for us with some pizzas, "to celebrate Gali's party, right,

Galush?" Pizza dinners were some of the most joyous moments for my children, and for me, too, if I'm being honest. A day without cooking and cleaning was a good day. I led everybody out to the garden to keep the party going. When Yairi asked how everything had gone, my mother gave him a long-winded account of the serendipity of meeting "Tzipi from the bus—and have you seen how handsome her son is and how sweet her grandson?"

Then she added, staring straight at me, "The handsome son seemed to have his eye on Maya. Maybe you should watch out, Yair." I was sure she hadn't noticed his interest. Yairi placed his hand on my shoulder and replied, "Then he must have excellent taste."

When the kids were in bed, Yair asked about Tzipi, and I told him about her romance with Itzhak; how his family had made Aliyah while hers immigrated to Canada and later to the United States; how, finally, she had found her way to Israel but hadn't found Itzhak; and how I was planning on reuniting the pair at the end of Shavuot. Yairi said in a half-joking, half-serious tone, "I hope her handsome son isn't planning on joining your excursion," and I replied with a wink that I hadn't even considered it, but now that he had broached the subject himself, perhaps Lior would in fact hop on the bandwagon. Yairi pulled me close to him, pressed his lips to mine, and my heart fluttered with backflips.

Chapter Forty-Three:
MAYA, 2019

EN ROUTE TO JERUSALEM

I had made arrangements to pick up Tzipke from her apartment in central Tel Aviv, but the evening before our trip she called and asked if there was room for Lior to join us. Her request surprised me and was understandable at the same time. On the one hand, I hadn't expected that her beloved, dazzlingly handsome son, the CEO of an esteemed advertising agency, would take a day off to join his mother on a trip to the nursing home of a long-lost love, but on the other hand, it made sense that her son would want to make sure she didn't get too excited and overstep her limits.

I agreed, and she suggested we meet at the entrance to the preschool, sparing me the morning drive around the big, traffic-jammed city. I called Itzhak to confirm the arrangement. He spoke a mile a minute, not pausing even for punctuation.

"Listen," he said, "I'm happy for Tzipke to come with her son, why should I let it bother me? I'm actually happy to meet him. But I'm also a bit worried. I'm pretty old now," he said bashfully, "and I'm not sure she'll like what she sees. You see, that's what I take issue with."

I smiled and thought it was funny how we're so concerned with our appearances, no matter what age or stage in life. I told Itzhak that it was okay because Tzipke wasn't young anymore, either, and the most important thing was for him to enjoy the momentous occasion and stop worrying—everything would be okay.

"Okay, you're right, I understand," Itzhak said, "but can I ask just one more thing of you?"

"Of course," I replied.

"I'd like you to inform Tzipke before she arrives that I am deaf, blind, and have cancer." His words lingered in the air.

"Why don't you tell her all that yourself?" I suggested, a bit stunned. I heard him coughing lightly.

"Listen, I'm really very old, and the last time we met I was in another world, we were both children. I don't want to hurt her in any way. She probably thinks I disappeared from her life and never even looked for her, even though I did, for many years. I searched and waited, until I couldn't do it anymore, and even though I married someone else, I never forgot about her. I don't expect you to tell her all that, only to prepare her for the fact that I'm old and sick, and not what I once was." After promising to prepare Tzipke for this seventy-year reunion, I reminded Itzhak again that she too had grown old, and that I firmly believed our hearts and perspective remained intact at any age.

After the kids fell asleep, I told Yairi about the back and forth between Tzipke and Itzhak I'd navigated that day. Yairi smiled and said that his takeaway from the story was that the hot dad who had once ogled me was joining our trip, and I shyly confirmed his theory, thinking in my heart that maybe a bit of jealousy wouldn't hurt him; his wife could also have suitors—even attractive ones. Yairi's affair, I tried to relegate to the back of my mind, and the fact that I still didn't know much about Ye'ela, not even how long their relationship had been going on, or how he'd truly felt. I knew that these were questions that would soon surface on their own.

I gazed at this man, who was gazing back at me with a sleepy smile and kissing the back of my neck. He looked so tired and imperfect, it actually made me long for him even more, which was enough to quash all my bitter thoughts, at least on that evening. I knew my ambitious curiosity wouldn't do me any good, not even if I knew every last detail. Nothing in life was certain, nothing was deserved or promised to any of us—a realization that was both stressful and liberating. To live in the moment, enjoy what is at our disposal, not be so disturbed by every little thing. "Don't forget to take a video," he added. "It's a wonderful memory to preserve for both of their families."

I woke up the next morning and organized the cameras. Before going to sleep, I'd made a list of questions to ask, and made sure my laptop was charged and ready to roll. After rushing to get the kids ready for school, I got myself ready and then looked in the mirror, not particularly liking the image looking back at me.

A new wrinkle had formed on my forehead, and I didn't like the checkered shirt I was wearing, so I changed into one that left my shoulder half exposed, then tossed it aside for a denim shirt, which left me just equally dissatisfied. After exchanging my jeans for white pants, I decided that they "made me look fat," finally opting for a white shirt with blue flowers, which I accessorized with a jeans jacket and a different pair of white pants that complimented my figure.

On the way to preschool, Gali was quiet, which is how I ended up listening, on the tape playing in car for the umpteenth time, to a story about Sammy the firefighter who was "a big hero, bigger than all of the other dads, but not as much of a hero as Aba Yairi." When we got out of the car and walked toward school, Gali's small hand folded into mine, and I saw Tzipke already waiting for us outside. From far away, she looked thirty years younger than her real age. As I approached, I could make out her wrinkles and her beautiful, bright eyes. I gave her a big hug.

She looked gorgeous in her white suit and colorful scarf wrapped around her neck. Saying that Lior and Matan were already at school, she smiled at Gali, and complimented my floral shirt. I thanked her, retook Gali's hand, and off we went into the school. Inside, Gali immediately ran toward Matan, saying, "Matan, I'm here, do you want to play in the doll area?" Without waiting for his response, she then ran to the teacher, who received her in a wide embrace, while I stood there watching, proud of my daughter's confidence, and of Sima, "the best teacher in the world, seriously the queen of preschools everywhere." Then I noticed Lior standing right in front of me, scanning me like an ultrasound machine; when I broke his stare with a "good morning," he smiled. We said goodbye to the kids and the teacher and left the building without exchanging a word. When we saw Tzipke, he offered her his elbow, which she took regally, and we all sauntered together toward my car. I looked at them with a hint of envy, unable to imagine linking arms with my own mother; something about their intimacy was so pleasant and comforting. Lior helped his mother into the front seat then went to sit in the back.

The road was congested on the way to Jerusalem, but the weather was ideal. Tzipke asked me to fill her in a bit more about the family story. Who ended up married to whom? How many kids had been born to each one of them? How many grandchildren? Were there any great grandchildren? I told her that Itzhak was really looking forward to seeing her, but that he was afraid he wouldn't recognize her, and even more uncertain that she would recognize him. "Take into account," I told her, "he's not young anymore or in good health."

Tzipke was silent and then said, "Seventy years. Definitely not a walk in the park. We've both been through so much in our lives, it will just be nice to see him and hear his story."

I smiled at her, and then looked in the mirror and saw Lior smiling, too, his dashing eyes once again piercing mine; and my heart did a backflip, which startled me. Breathing deeply, I focused on the twisting road.

By the time we began the ascent to Jerusalem through the valley, our conversation had already become quite involved. We spoke about nature and art, about the fact that although no one in my family was a Holocaust survivor, the stories from that traumatic time affected all of us, and antisemitism in the world would never truly go away; on the contrary, in some places it was only getting worse. Then we switched topics and spoke about Tzipke's family.

I was enjoying the ride so much, I didn't want it to end, but my curiosity somehow made me drive faster, and then Tzipke said, "That war was only the first. We thought if we survived it, we wouldn't have to endure any more disasters because we had been victims for long enough. We didn't think for a moment that it wasn't over yet." Lior squeezed her shoulder, and she put her hand over his and said, "We arrived in Canada and the great United States. In neither place were we licking honey, if you know what I mean. If you remember, my parents had lost a baby when the war started, that was already on Sunday after the expulsion, but you know what, let's let it be, I don't want to talk about it, I just want to say that when my eldest brother decided to come to Israel, my parents followed in his footsteps, and so did I. Then we lost my brother Lolek, bless his soul, in the Six-Day War. My parents lost two children to war, and they died of grief, so I could do nothing but hold onto this ground with all my might, until this very day."

Goosebumps rose on my arms and the back of my neck. I looked at Lior and said, "I'm so sorry to hear that. I didn't know."

"Yes," Tzipke said. "During the war we lost my little brother, and almost our entire family. Those who were left in Poland ended up in the camps, and those who were exiled to Russia didn't all survive. We lost uncles, aunts, cousins, grandparents, and at the end of the war, only my parents, my older brother Lolek, and my brother Shmulik were left. That's it."

"What brought you to Israel?" I asked, and she replied: "Lolek insisted we make Aliyah in the mid-fifties, and my parents couldn't bear the thought of separating from him, so they decided that we would all go together. We didn't think for a moment what the future had in store."

I looked at her wrinkles, the suffering etched on her face, every line signifying an experience from her life—hardship, loss, but also laughter. She had never lost her spirit, or her optimism. For a moment, I was ashamed that the small wrinkle I'd discovered earlier that day had caused me to feel out of sorts; maybe I needed to be thankful for it, this experience I had earned. Nothing should be taken for granted, neither overcoming our problems nor old age, which is a gift that not everybody receives.

I thought about Holocaust survivors, about the plights they faced over the course of their lives and couldn't fathom how they had done it. Then it hit me—the stillbirth I had endured between Dana and Gali. There was nothing more terrible than losing a child, that constricting feeling of emptiness inside. I hadn't allowed the thought to haunt me in years, but neither had I ever completely healed from the experience.

When I had returned home after the stillbirth, I promised myself two things: I would have another child and our home would continue to be joyful, despite the loss.

We drove in silence, each one of us absorbed in our own thoughts. I had lost one child, gone through a serious crisis, and lived to tell the tale. Tzipke's parents had lost two children. How could any optimism remain after so much loss?

I felt my lost child flickering in and out of the vacuum of infinity, staying just long enough to offer me a consoling hug, his presence so visceral. Maybe he was watching over us, and maybe he was the reason my sweet Gali had come into this world because I hadn't wanted more than three children to begin with. My thoughts and emotions a cloudy whirlpool, I suddenly wanted to hug the child back, thank him, tell him I hadn't meant any harm, that not everything was under our control. Life had a tendency to change form and size, and in the midst of all of it, we are merely busy-bodied ants in this atomic space with which the world may choose to cooperate or beat down with all its might. Trying to hide the tears sprouting from my eyes, I said, "Darn, I think I missed the turn to the nursing home. We'll have to make a U-turn."

Chapter Forty-Four: ITZHAK, MARCH 1944

KAZAKHSTAN

When we reached Kazakhstan toward the end of 1943, we lived temporarily in a single room, in the house of a family who agreed to host us in exchange for some extra bread. For a short period, we moved between apartments, warehouses, and sometimes even train stations, when we were unable to find a family to host us for the night. When Father left the hospital, we stayed with an especially friendly family, but soon they could no longer continue hosting us, and we were on the move yet again.

The Russians provided us with a cabin of sorts—finally, a house that was just for us, where we could feel as though we were at home, and not be banished at any given moment. The "house," if we can call it that, was warmed by fertilizer made of cow manure and smeared all over the walls, producing an awful smell. We weren't freezing in the Zamlinka, but the living conditions certainly weren't too pleasant. The first time I entered the place, all I could perceive was a large, stinky room. In the corner, there was a kind of oven, in the opposite corner a chimney, and the rest of the space was to be used for sleeping and sitting around. While Father got a fire going, Mother and my sisters arranged our few belongings. We nibbled on our daily bread quietly within the four walls of our new house. At least we weren't freezing, and we had a roof above our heads to protect us from the terrible cold, and we were all together, which always gave us more strength than anything else.

During that period, Father began to work in a gold mine. Along with the other miners, he was lowered into the belly of the earth, where they dug for hours before being lifted back to the surface to sift through the pebbles and look for precious ores. It was strenuous work and full of dust. There were days when it was hard for Father to breathe, but he persevered through his pain in order to provide us with the few bites of bread or potato at the end of a day's work.

Chapter Forty-Five:
MAYA, 2019

JERUSALAM

When we got to the nursing home, Itzhak, wearing a blue suit that flattered his glowing face, waited for us at the entrance. Tzipke walked toward him carefully, and they both smiled and embraced before the tears began flowing. Speaking affectionately in Yiddish, they kept reaching in for another hug, gazing at one another in disbelief. When they had finished their tearful embraces, Tzipke turned to us and said: "It is a real wonder to be standing here at this moment, and who would have thought that we would meet again one day after so many years." Lior and I couldn't hold back our tears, either.

"Come meet my son. This is Lior, he's an only child," Tzipke said. Lior approached Itzhak and shook his hand. Then they hugged.

Itzhak told Lior, "You have your mother's beautiful eyes." Unable to hide his emotion, he turned to me for confirmation. I replied that he was correct, they both did have beautiful eyes. Tzipke blushed and thanked me for the compliment, and for arranging the meeting, "which never would have happened without you." Then I realized I hadn't gotten any pictures, so I took my camera out of my bag and snapped a photo of them standing in front of a rosebush that seemed to be blooming especially for the occasion. The three smiled broadly at the camera, and afterward, I took a picture of Itzhak and Tzipke together, for posterity.

When I had taken enough photographs to fill an album, I asked Itzhak if he wanted to go to a nearby café—the one we'd sat at together so many times before. He was happy to, as was Tzipke. Lior and I walked together, and Itzhak and Tzipke in front of us, Itzhak supporting Tzipke on his arm; if I hadn't known the background story, I would have thought they were just another elderly couple out for their daily stroll. My heart skipped a beat. Would Yairi and I be walking like that in our old age?

I smiled at Lior, who said, "I really appreciate you putting this meeting together." He smiled broadly. "My mother hasn't smiled like this since my father passed away. She's very lonely."

Inside the café, a friendly waitress approached us and led us to our table. As we sat down, Itzhak held out his hand to Tzipke and said, "Seventy years, and your blue eyes still shine in the exact same way."

And she said, "You thought I wouldn't recognize you, but it was too easy, your facial structure is exactly the same, and your sharp nose gave it all away."

We all burst out laughing, and Tzipke leaned on Itzhak for a moment and added, "Even if I hadn't seen you my entire life, I would recognize you in the next one, because that's what happens when souls are intertwined, you just know each other." Then she added, almost in a whisper, "The heart always remembers."

After being granted permission to record the meeting, I took out my video camera and told everyone they would be able to view the entire reel at the book launch celebration of Itzhak's life story. Tzipke, who took interest in my various projects, nodded and said that she would be honored to participate in such an extraordinary initiative. "Aside from Ichu's family's story"—that's what she called him as though they were still children—"and our own, it's so important to bear witness to the Holocaust. Soon there won't be anybody left to do it," she said quietly. Itzhak agreed with her and clasped her hands. Lior and I looked at them in admiration, and I hoped that this young couple would be able to enjoy many more years of good health together.

Tzipke interrogated Itzhak about his family: "What happened after they were separated? Did everybody make Aliyah? When did they get married? How many children did everybody have? How many grandchildren? Great-grandchildren?" Itzhak answered each question patiently, narrating the story of his journey to Israel in great detail, mentioning the small apartment they had lived in after leaving the absorption center in Ramleh, and the fact that his parents had lived to a ripe old age, long enough to meet their grandchildren and great-grandchildren. Itzhak told us that his brother Shimon, who had been a strong, healthy swimming champion, had died suddenly, from a tragic, unexpected heart attack, that Shifra had suffered many years of debilitating depression, and about the loss of Sima—his sister and last remaining sibling—a few years ago. Then he asked Tzipke about her life in America, confessing that he had thought about her tirelessly while on his own trip to America with his children when they had been exploring the possibility of immigrating there themselves.

Tzipke said that although they'd lived for a period of time in America, her brother Lolek had insisted on making Aliyah and joining the army, where he was later killed in the Six-Day War. Itzhak said he was sorry to hear about Lolek's death, and I could see that he was struggling to accept the reality of it. "He was such a sweet, handsome boy," he murmured, and asked if he had managed to raise a family before he died. "Yes, he was married to Edith, who passed away a few years ago, and their children, Ohad and Yossi, are both so wonderful, they were so young when he died—five and three years old. And my parents were brokenhearted, so I married Ahar'le, to lift their spirits and give them grandchildren."

Itzhak wiped a tear from his eye and said, "Your family endured so much, it's really inconceivable." Then he said that he hadn't heard anything about their family since they were separated from each other, but that while visiting Brooklyn he had looked for her all over. "Millions of people pass through the streets of Brooklyn, and I was convinced I might see you there," he blushed. Tzipke smiled and asked what year they had been there, since they had returned to Israel in 1977, and he looked at her and said, "That's so funny, I was in Brooklyn in the spring of 1977," and she smiled and said, "When we got married in 1962, my husband Ahar'le, may his memory be a blessing, dreamed of going to America for his doctorate. There was a special psychology program in New York, with the best psychoanalysts of the time, and I, who wasn't so keen on going, agreed, thinking that I ought to make the sacrifice for him. So we went, agreeing not to stay past his studies, because it wasn't easy on my parents, either, who were already quite old, plus I wanted to raise my children in Israel. We ended up staying for almost ten years, until the Yom Kippur War started, and I became sick with worry.

Ahar'le flew to Israel to enlist, and I went along with him and lived with my parents. After the war, we returned to New York, where Ahar'le tried to convince me to stay, and we argued about it endlessly. When Lior was born, it was in America," Tzipke said and smiled at her son, saying that she eventually managed to convince her husband that despite the difficulties in Israel, "It's our country, we'll never be banished from there, and we'll never be called dirty Jews." That summer, she returned to Israel, after Ahar'le, may his memory be a blessing, had become highly successful in his field, his reputation making its way to Tel Aviv University, where he was offered tenure as a professor, "which finally put an end to his excuses." Tzipke burst out laughing, and we laughed along with her. Finally, back in Israel, they bought a small apartment near the sea; while her husband taught at the university, she worked at a travel agency, and "life just passed so quickly."

Tzipke was quiet for a moment, took a sip of tea, and said, "So what happened when you went to America? Did you end up moving there?"

Itzhak shook his head. He had been received as a guest of honor by his relatives, some of whom he had never even met, and some of whom he had last seen in the DP camp. When he arrived in Brooklyn, he fell in love with the place and wanted to stay, but his wife, an immigrant herself, refused to hear of it, since she didn't want to be disconnected from her family and strike roots in yet another foreign place.

"I have to ask you something," Tzipke suddenly said to Itzhak.

"Yes?" Itzhak's leg bounced up and down, as if preparing to field a painful question.

"When we were separated all the way back in Heidenheim, when we left and you stayed, it was so hard for me, and I knew it was for you, too, because I understood your heart best out of everyone's…" Lior and I fidgeted uncomfortably, and Itzhak looked as though he was suffocating, but none of it fazed Tzipke. It seemed as though she had waited her entire life to ask the question on the tip of her tongue. Looking into Itzhak's eyes, she said, "Itzhak, you promised me when we separated, on that day, that you'd never forget me—and let me tell you, I shed more tears that day than I did my entire life—but you promised that you'd come after me and find me, no matter where I went, that's what you said, and you promised you'd marry me."

The three of us sat there for a long time waiting for Itzhak's answer.

Then Itzhak replied quietly, "I fulfilled my promise over the years. I looked for you in every way possible: through mutual friends, through the radio program that reunited loved ones; I even called and begged them to look for you and your family, but I couldn't find you anywhere, Tzipke. I'm so sorry that's how it turned out, and I hope you'll be able to forgive me one day but believe me when I say I tried my best to find you, and when I lost hope, I was already thirty, my parents were pressuring me to get married, and I met my wife at the factory in which we both worked. But I never forgot you." Holding his face, he burst into tears, and she held his hand, saying that it was tragic he hadn't been able to find her and vice versa, probably because she'd lived abroad for so many years, and afterward, she felt that finding him would be a betrayal to her husband, so she stopped looking.

I checked to make sure the video camera was still running. I had not only documented the life stories of these two cherished people, which would teach their family members so much about their past and current lives, but also showed their present state: their unfaltering humanity, their disappointment, their joys, and hardships. After Itzhak and Tzipke had opened up, Itzhak suggested showing Tzipke his current living arrangements and asked if we, "the children," wanted to accompany them. Lior and I suggested that they go on their own.

Tzipke and Itzhak rose from their seats, and we walked them to the nursing home. From there, Lior and I began strolling through the German Colony, which was eerily quiet for the middle of the week. Lior's presence was no longer threatening—it turned out that this handsome man wasn't only handsome, but also a lover of history and geography, and we enjoyed talking to each other. I daresay he had even taken a liking to me, but I knew that Yairi and three cute kids were waiting for me at home, and I was happy that my emotional state had stabilized. Who knows what might have happened if I had gone on a stroll with Lior when Yairi and I were on bad terms? That thought entered my brain for a split second but was quickly replaced by another one: What doesn't kill you makes you stronger, and we learn from every one of our experiences, no matter how difficult.

Chapter Forty-Six: ICHU, MARCH 1944

KAZAKHSTAN

That morning, there was no one in the Zamlinka. I woke up to the usual stench, lying on the bare floor. A few coals were left over from the night before, offering up some heat to the freezing room. Grandpa had already gone—I had no idea to where—Mother was probably standing in line for bread, and Father had long since left for work. My sisters were already at school, and Shimon at the factory. I was happy that no one was around and went out to look for some trouble to keep me busy for the day.

It was freezing outside, but not more than usual. I hoped that Shimon would be able to snag a pair of boots for me, like the ones he had brought for Shifra and Sima. I was so jealous of them, but I didn't say a word. Shimon promised me that I would be next, adding that I should just wait patiently, and I understood what he meant. Being a girl was hard, and Father always taught us to be gentlemen, to treat women the way he treated our own mother, so I waited patiently for my turn. In the meantime, two whole weeks had passed, and every time Shimon came home, I hoped he'd be holding those boots behind his back, and I wouldn't have to wear my worn-out shoes any longer.

I was sick of begging for change in this cold. There were a million kids just like me, standing and asking for money, and very few people had any to spare. The war had pulled everyone into poverty. Whenever I passed by a pretty house, the smell of grilled meat wafting from its windows, I stood there for a few minutes just to take it in, imagining the people sitting inside and eating, thinking of how full they must be, their clothes prim and proper, wearing shoes without any holes, immune to the snow and cold.

When I went outside wearing my mother's clothes, the ones she had patched together for me, a little girl looked at me and asked in Russian, "Are you a boy or a girl?" I almost cried, but instead told her to scram, so that she'd figure out the answer herself. I went to look for Sasha and the gang. They were standing by a potato stand, looking at the potatoes as though they were Hanukkah candles, only to be observed, not touched. When Sasha saw me, he whispered, "Let's see you steal a potato. If you do it, I'll give you a quarter of a ruble." I didn't really believe that he'd give me anything, but Sasha knew he could trust me, and sometimes even gave me a branch to add to our fire, so I tried to behave my best around him.

I told him that as usual, he could count on me, but instead of a quarter of a ruble, I wanted a cigarette. Even a used one would do. Since I'd started smoking, I was always after that garbage, even though it was so hard to find. He said first I had to bring him the potato, and then we'd talk. Sasha knew that my childlike face could get me out of a lot of tight situations.

When I approached the stand, people were crowded around it. The stand owner barely noticed me. Grabbing a potato from the side of the stand, I made my getaway before anybody could say anything. Sasha was right, I wasn't bad at all. Of course, there was no quarter of a ruble. We split that pathetic potato, each taking a small bite, imagining we were eating a bowl full of mashed potatoes topped with caramelized onions, resting over a plate of thick meat smothered in sauce.

Chapter Forty-Seven: MAYA, 2019

TEL AVIV

The ride home was fairly quiet. Tzipke still seemed to be processing her emotions, Lior didn't say much, and neither did I. I thought about the next chapters I'd write, and about the fact that I had captured some pretty fantastic documentary moments during their meeting. I considered what I could do with them, the obvious option being a screening during the family party I'd organize at the end of the project.

I knew that I would meet with Itzhak and Tzipke separately again, but I also had to fill in some gaps, especially the years they had spent apart. There were so many Holocaust narratives, as well as endless stories of love and its disappointments, but something like this, a separation of seventy years, how many such stories had been documented? I thought about the courses of both of their lives, each on their own journey, which took place in a parallel world—marriages to different partners, work, careers, births, additional losses, bodies that betrayed the passage of time, the clock ticking faster and faster until suddenly this miracle of a reunion.

At the Sha'ar HaGuy intersection, Yairi called to ask how the visit had gone. I told him how wonderful it had been, and I'd make it back in time to pick up Gali. I'd tell him the details at home.

I dropped off Lior and Tzipke near the preschool. With a hug, Tzipke thanked me warmly. "If it weren't for you, none of this would have happened. Thank you for bringing Ichu and me together," she said. I told her that it meant the world to me, and that I'd be in touch again soon.

Lior also hugged and thanked me. We went into the preschool, where Lior gave Matan a hug. Gali ran up to me, and I hugged and kissed her soft cheeks, thanking the universe for the great gift I'd been given.

The next day, after the kids and Yairi left the house, I sat down at the computer. Thoughts swirled together in my mind, historical facts merging with people I'd written about, strengthening my sense of purpose. I'd tell this story from beginning to end, trying my best not to miss a thing, I promised myself. And the next chapter rolled off my fingers.

In the evening, after the kids had gone to bed, Yair and I planned our trip to Holland. We booked hotels and plane tickets, mapped out our route through the country, and chose activities that looked interesting. As we planned, I felt our connection growing, and we went upstairs to our queen bed and made love. Life was more beautiful than ever—sleeping beside the man I loved, waking up in the morning to my children—what more did one need? Still, something in my heart felt incomplete.

Chapter Forty-Eight: ITZHAK, MARCH 1944

KAZAKHSTAN

My older sister Shifra was a strong, kindhearted girl. Anytime somebody needed help, Shifra was the first to show up. Whenever I was sad, she took on my laughter as her mission. If somebody didn't feel well, Shifra would run to get help. Mother always knew that she could trust her with anything.

I won't ever forget that morning. Each one of us had already gone off to do our own thing, just as we did every morning—Father to the gold mine, Mother to the woodchopper to retrieve wood for the Zamlinka, Shimon to the factory, and Shifra and Grandpa to fetch the daily bread. We received only three hundred grams of bread per person. Beyond that, we didn't eat anything, sometimes for months on end. The bread kept us alive, but just barely.

That day, when Shifra's turn came, she received a loaf of bread for us, in addition to the ration slips for the rest of the week. Heading back home, she noticed a group of boys following her. Shifra sped up, and at a certain point, began running, the boys close behind, until they caught up with her and pushed her to the ground, demanding the bread. Shifra defended it fiercely, tucking it inside her boot, but to no avail—the loaf was taken from her, and the ration slips along with it.

Shifra came home bruised and weeping, and when Mother understood what had happened, she whacked her on the head. We wouldn't have any food for the rest of the week. Fuming, Mother left the house and set out for the sunflower oil factory she'd recently heard about. She'd been told that if you went there at the end of the day, the tattered remains of the sunflowers were for the taking. She ran to the neighboring village, a few kilometers away from our Zamlinka and begged the factory owners for some scraps, explaining that our ration slips and weekly bread portion had been stolen, and that in the harsh winter, we stood little chance of survival because everything was frozen, there were no forest berries or fish, nothing at all. The factory owner took pity on my mother and gave her the leftover stock, from which oil could be sucked, as well as crushed sunflowers, typically fed to animals. Mother piled all of it onto her back and brought it home for us. When Father returned from work and heard what had happened, he went out to look for Mother, and when he saw her, he ran toward her, embraced her and said, "Chaya, my love, my wife, I am so thankful that the Lord gave you to me as a gift, and for everything you do for our family." The crushed sunflowers saved our lives that week, until the next time we received ration slips. Mother didn't let Shifra bring home the bread anymore, but made sure to wait in line herself, hiding the loaf and ration slips close to her heart.

Eventually, Mother found work cleaning someone's house. Father, who could no longer bear the weight of the heavy sacks on his back, or the horrible dust that was the source of his respiratory problems, left the gold mine, telling the manager that he was a shoemaker by trade. The two of them, my mother and father, as well as Shimon, began bringing home a salary, which was more than just leftover food, but we couldn't do much with the money, since barely anything was being sold at the regular market, and on the black market, the prices were too high.

Chapter Forty-Nine: MAYA, 2019

TEL AVIV

A few weeks had passed since Tzipke and Lior's visit to Itzhak's nursing home, and I had found time to sit with each of them to document the divergent paths they had taken with their families. Whenever I went to visit Itzhak, I found him sitting cozily in his small room, his hearing aid at the ready, listening to the radio. He always kept up with what was going on around him, and we even chatted about the upcoming elections at the start of our conversation.

Sometimes, an English word would slip into his sentences. He had learned the language many years earlier, while considering immigration to America. While the idea never came into being, he fell in love with the language. Whenever he accidentally said a word in English, he would smile bashfully, and I would smile back. His youthful charm accompanied him everywhere.

Regardless of the season, Itzhak always offered me a cup of tea with lemon. Steaming mugs in hand, we would sit on his small balcony overlooking clusters of buildings and take in the fresh Jerusalem air. Once I asked him how it was to live in Israel when for years the country didn't formally recognize his suffering and that of his family. With a red face, he replied, "Insolent scumbags! We weren't recognized as Holocaust survivors because we were spared the death camps. Do you know what we went through, what scars we had to carry with us for decades afterward?" Itzhak touched my shoulder, as if trying to convince me—as if I needed convincing. "Hunger and suffering, death, terrible cold, the loss of loved ones who haven't been buried to this day. If I wanted to go to my Aunt Hasya's grave, may her memory be a blessing, I wouldn't be able to find it," he said in frustration. "She was buried in the forests of the Russian steppe, my grandmother in some godforsaken place along the way, without even a gravestone, and my Aunt Zelda next to some village whose name I don't even know."

"During the first years after the war," Itzhak recounted, "when the payments for Holocaust survivors began pouring in, despite my parents' dire financial situation, they refused to pay them a cent after Hitler had taken nearly my father's entire family and some of my mother's. No financial compensation would be enough to make up for those horrible years and incomprehensible losses. But after my parents passed, my brother put in a request for compensation, and it was denied, on the grounds that the war we endured was in Russian territory, not in the Nazi extermination or labor camps."

Feeling Itzhak's pain, I said something I had wanted to say to him for a long time. "Who has the right to decide who is a survivor and who isn't? There are so many parties to consider—the country, relatives, friends, and acquaintances. Who gets to decide who receives reparations, and who doesn't? How can one measure another's suffering? It's an impossible task."

Itzhak nodded. "I have nightmares to this day, more than seventy years after the end of the war, and I'm unable to deal with hunger or cold. I don't need to convince anyone of what I went through," he said. Turning his face toward the sky, he added, "Only God and man know the extent of human suffering."

Itzhak's wisdom was profound and painful, and I tried to calm the storm of anger that had suddenly emerged from his gentle soul, but to no avail. It was as though I had opened a Pandora's box. He continued. "The Holocaust hounds all those who endured it, whether in a camp or 'only' in exile. The Holocaust never ended; it pursues us survivors with every step we take, and our children and grandchildren. The trauma hasn't ended yet and won't end anytime soon."

Maybe in a few generations it will turn into something else, I thought, and we will be able to look at the Holocaust as "merely" an historical event that must never happen again. But as long as survivors are with us, and the children and grandchildren of survivors, the trauma of the Holocaust will still infect their daily lives, and the soul will find no peace.

"The reparations that streamed in from Germany for decades never reached a large segment of the survivors," Itzhak continued. "One of the reasons was that the country simply didn't want to share the large sums of money it had received with the survivors, who were getting old as it was. My siblings began to receive compensation only two decades ago. At first, it was only Shimon, who managed to track down the right forms, but neither I nor my sisters could get our hands on them. That minister Silvan Shalom decided that whoever returned to Germany after the war wasn't eligible for a penny. But we didn't have anywhere to go! Nowhere!" Itzhak said in exasperation, as though still pleading his case, so many years later. "When we returned to Poland, we were pelted with rocks and not allowed to get off the train, so we continued to a DP camp in Germany, and from there we made Aliyah to Israel. That was why we weren't eligible for compensation, according to Silvan Shalom." Itzhak gazed at me helplessly before continuing. "It was only in 2002 that we were finally considered eligible. At least it came with my old age and made life a little bit easier. But let's leave it alone," he said with a wave of his hand. "It was in the government's interest to keep the money that was funneled directly to them. They benefited from making the lives of us survivors difficult. A double injustice."

Softly, I said, "I'm so sorry. I didn't mean to anger you. Let's go out for a walk, and you can tell me about your last year in Kazakhstan."

Chapter Fifty:
ICHU, APRIL 1944

KAZAKHSTAN

During the day, when everybody else was busy, I was out with my gang. We got into a lot of mischief, which made me pretty popular. They waited for me in the morning next to my Zamlinka, and we strolled around together. On one such outing to the market, we found a long stick and rammed a nail into it. As always, I was assigned the most daring task. I held out the stick as far as it could go, until it pierced a juicy apple, and then pulled it back toward me. The stand owner, who knew exactly what was going on, tried running after me, but my good friends clung to his clothing, slowing him down, while I made my getaway, apple in hand.

We couldn't believe our triumph! The leader of the gang, Yvgeny, praised my success, bit his buck teeth into the apple until there was nothing left for me. "Tomorrow," Yvgeny said, "tomorrow, I'll make sure to leave half the apple for you." But that almost never happened; there's always somebody more important who deserved a bigger bite than me since I'm so small, and "You don't even need to eat that much," Yvgeny told me, and then he added, "Small as you are, you're a big rascal, aren't you?" I know that's not something he tells just anybody because Yvgeny, as our strong, tough leader, couldn't go around giving everybody compliments. Plus, I'm the one he sends out on all the missions that require somebody "small and speedy."

Yvgeny trusted me and called me a "little demon." Sometimes he lifted me onto his wide shoulders, and we marched through the streets of Dajlimbrad like two heroes who could even be brothers. One time, Yvgeny told me that if I stole Grandpa's tobacco cup, which he had earned after a whole week of sewing for some family "who had everything they needed and more," and gave Yvgeny the tobacco, he would give me a pair of skates in exchange. Owning a pair of skates was a big dream of mine. There's nothing, besides maybe some good meat or some really dense bread, that would make me happier than to skate around town, like some of the other kids in the gang.

I was so excited that I planned the mission perfectly. "It's just a small mission, nothing serious," Yvgeny said. When Grandpa wasn't paying attention, I took his cup and stuffed it deep inside the pocket of Mother's dress that Grandpa had sewn into a pair of pants for me. Nobody noticed, and I snuck out of the house and handed the cup to Yvgeny proudly.

"You little rascal, those innocent eyes aren't fooling anyone," he said, his own eyes glowing. Just as he had promised, he gave me a pair of skates, and I spent the rest of the day skating around happily. What wasn't very fun was at the end of the day he took the skates back, and when I protested that taking them back wasn't part of our agreement, he said with a serious expression, "Did I ever tell you the skates would be yours forever? I said I would give them to you, and there, I gave them to you for a whole day, so don't start crying and whining about what we agreed on, all right?" Of course, I didn't say anything, I just left, praying in my heart that Grandpa wouldn't find out who took his beloved tobacco cup from right under his nose. He didn't ever find out, but when he saw that the cup was missing, he was angry, mostly at himself, thinking that he had probably left it at the house where he had worked or some other place.

Chapter Fifty-One: MAYA, 2019

TEL AVIV

I met with Itzhak as often as I could in the following weeks, catalyzing my research process. Yairi and I had planned our trip to Holland down to the last detail, including sleeping arrangements in a national park adjacent to one of the canals that traversed the country. I tried to make progress with my writing, but it was hard to focus. Summer had begun, and in a few weeks, the kids would already be on vacation.

Things with Yairi were slowly improving. We went back to consulting one another about things just as we had done for years, sharing our thoughts and feelings, but the fact that I hadn't asked, and he hadn't divulged too much information about his fleeting romance still made me queasy, as much as I tried to push it away, to forgive and forget.

Our "holy grail"—our set-in-stone weekly dates—became more enjoyable as time went by. We spoke for hours on end, and Noga, our babysitter, was pleased with these Tuesday night gigs. Yairi always showed up at our planned meeting spot on time and without any fuss.

We went out to shows, cafes, sometimes to a movie or to friends, anything that would make both of us happy and remind us of the sanctity of our partnership. When I told Anat that I still hadn't raised the painful questions with Yairi that I had been averse to asking, she posed two questions of her own: Why was I leaving the things that bothered me to fester and would I feel better after hearing all the details?

I didn't know the answer to either question, and we agreed that I would think about them and come back in a week. Over the next few days, I found myself staring at Yairi, and asking myself where I had disappeared to and why. Were the answers to Anat's questions a more precise mirror to what was going on inside me than what was going on around me?

Anat reminded me, as she always did before we wrapped up our meeting, of my tendency to please others while forgetting myself in the process. Did the answer lie somewhere there, I asked myself? Anat reminded me not to forgo quality time with myself, and I waited for those hours expectantly. Sometimes I met a friend for coffee, or I went to the library, where I would sit quietly, undisturbed. At other times, I strolled the streets of Tel Aviv or took in an exhibit at a museum.

Tel Aviv had become my second home, and so much friendlier than the city I had known from my childhood. I discovered anew the charm of the alleyways and found I wasn't bad at striking up conversations with complete strangers. Whenever I returned home from these adventures, I was already anticipating the next, which gave me a feeling of fulfillment and renewal.

Two days ago, on our weekly date, Yairi told me with a smile that he noticed something in me had changed. Surprised, I asked what exactly, and he said something in me had aroused his curiosity, and he looked forward to dissecting it from up close. He laughed as I smiled; it was interesting that what he identified as a change was in reality just me being my true self. The only difference was that I had made a point of emphasizing my own importance in the grand chaos that was our family.

I decided the time had finally come for the "painful questions," and I told Yairi that when we had spoken that time in the café, and afterward at home when he'd returned to living with me and the children, he had actually told me very little about the affair, and I had promised myself that I would stay quiet, since there was no guarantee that I would be able to live with his answers; yet, it still bothered me and made it difficult to entirely forgive him.

His expression changed, and he said, "What good will the details do? Why is it even important? I thought you forgave me, and we had already moved on."

"I did, and we have, but it's still eating me up," I replied. Looking into his eyes, I said, "It's possible that your answers won't make me totally Zen about the whole thing, but at least I'll know I did everything in my power to understand, forgive, and try to get closer to you, truly closer." My words didn't work on Yair. Abruptly, he said that he had hoped "the whole thing was behind us already, and why are you trying to revive it? It's too exhausting, Maya, do you really think we'll be able to move on? How can I know if what I tell you will do anything to improve things?"

Staring at him, with no answer forthcoming, I said, "Maybe I never really will forgive you. Is that what you wanted to hear?" Yair rose from his seat, declaring that he wanted to go home. We paid the check and drove home, the cold wind of our relationship accompanying us the whole way.

***

I spent the following days immersed in my work and the needs of my children. The writing process had become more involved than I'd expected. The memories weren't always easy for Itzhak to share and revisiting that dark period of his life was a stressful undertaking for him. The last time I'd gone to meet him, I'd arrived early, and when I knocked on his door, I was surprised to discover that he wasn't in his room.

When I asked the staff where he'd gone, they responded with a wink that a well-dressed elderly woman had been seen with him that morning, and they'd left the nursing home not too long ago. I hoped and suspected that Tzipke might be the culprit. I knew that she could drive, but all the way from Tel Aviv to Jerusalem, at her age? That woman was really larger than life. Taking out my laptop, I sat in the lounge and waited for Itzhak to return.

I called Yairi and told him I was still waiting for Itzhak, who seemed to have forgotten that I was coming since he'd been seen leaving the nursing home with a well-dressed woman who I assumed was Tzipke, and if it really was Tzipke, then I had really "hit two birds with one stone." As I was about to finish the call, the two birds appeared, overjoyed to see me. I stood up and hugged them both, overcome with a feeling of warmth. Itzhak apologized profusely for forgetting our meeting but assured me that he was happy I had come, as always.

We entered his room and sat down next to the small table. Tzipke offered me some hot, sweet tea with lemon, and I responded that "there's nothing like hot, sweet tea with lemon in the middle of a boiling summer," knowing full well what her reply would be. "Hot, sweet tea is essential at any time of the year, especially with a slice of lemon." The two birds I'd captured looked giddy and younger than ever, their eyes glowing. Even in old age, eyes always reveal a story, absorbing the layers of one's life under their lids.

They told me they had taken a taxi tour around Jerusalem, trying to cherish every minute left together, filling in the gaps, enjoying each other's company. At their request, the driver had dropped them off at a small café in Yemin Moshe, overlooking the Tower of David and the walls of the Old City. "We sat there chatting as if not a single day had passed," Tzipke said with the excitement of a little girl. Itzhak smiled with a love I'd never seen before in his eyes, nodded and said, "It was too short, we must meet again." And Tzipke agreed.

Chapter Fifty-Two: ITZHAK, JUNE 2019

JERUSALEM

The nursing home is always especially warm in the summertime. In June, a heat wave the likes of which I had never experienced washed over Jerusalem. The air conditioner didn't always work, nor did an open window or door provide me much comfort. I tried to stick to my daily routine, which somehow helps me get through each day unharmed. Documenting my family's story is of the utmost importance to me. In a sense, it is also a race against time. Which one of us will come out alive? I might, with a bit of time to spare, or else the damned cancer spreading ruthlessly through my body will come out on top. "Memories build up like ants," wrote the poet Yona Volloch, and my memory—ants, ants, loading crumbs upon crumbs, transforming them into a home and paving the way for the next generations.

Maya didn't come today. I sat hunched over my desk and wrote to her. I'm lucky that these days, emails can be composed in Braille, which is then converted into written script. These technological wonders aid me in this collective mission Maya and I are on. I sailed to my last year in Kazakhstan, to the last winter in which my clothes were unbearably thin, and I walked the snowy streets coatless. My heroic brother Shimon saved us that winter. He was a hero because he was a seventeen-year-old boy suffering from malnutrition yet worked day and night to provide for our family, and that of Mordechai, who had joined the army, leaving behind a number of extra mouths to feed at our pitifully empty table. Shimon sewed boots for the soldiers on the front but also found the time to sew warm boots for his family, which helped us avoid hypothermia on our walks outside the Zamlinka. But when summer came around, we discovered to our dismay that it was still dry and cold.

Siberia was Siberia, in short, even though we had gone south to Kazakhstan. At that point, my parents had fairly regular work, Grandpa was repairing clothes and shoes alike, and a bit of meager bread was set on our table every night. Father had to leave the gold mine on account of his pulmonary problems caused by the mine's awful dust, and as a result, he became skilled at repairing whatever demanded repair: shoes, clothing, small carpentry tasks, or anything else.

The girls studied at school, and I, who had been left to my own devices, became quite the mischievous ragamuffin; but in the evening, we all gathered at home, to the same small room that stunk of cow manure, yet still appeared like a castle in our eyes. I remember our last year there, and what enters my mind immediately is the image of our nosy neighbor, who entered our Zamlinka one day, looked around her, crossed her arms and said to Grandpa, "I must admit, you really do have quite a God. The fact that your grandchildren are standing on their two feet with a smile after this winter is a tell-tale sign that He exists."

Grandpa considered her and said, "Our God is yours, too, and He is compassionate and merciful, He feeds and supports us, and He helps our children when they choose to help themselves."

She looked back at him, growled something indistinct, then whipped around and left. We all burst out laughing, and Grandpa added that he couldn't help but notice the envy in her eyes. We couldn't stop laughing. I remember it to this day. In general, we always preserved a sense of humor and optimism, even in our darkest moments.

Chapter Fifty-Three: ICHU, FEBRUARY 1945

KAZAKHSTAN

In the middle of the night, the Cossacks came to Shimon, my brother, who was sleeping at the edge of the room. "Samion, Samion, get up, get up!" they ordered him. I didn't understand what they were doing in our Zamlinka, nor what they could possibly want from Shimon, but Father whispered to me in Yiddish not to worry, they only wanted him to go to the factory to manufacture a pair of boots. Shimon got up and went after them.

When he came back, it was already morning. He told us they had bribed the guard at the entrance, gone inside the factory with him, given Shimon some wool and asked him to make a pair of boots for them. In exchange, they promised to give him a sack of durum. "A sack of durum?" I asked Grandpa. "What's that?" Grandpa explained that those were the pellets we'd received in Camp 19, the ones that had been similar to wheat, and that if we really received a sack, I wouldn't be hungry for at least seven days, if not longer. I was so happy I could have danced, but then I looked at how exhausted Shimon was. He said there was no time for him to sleep since he had to go back to the factory for his workday. I wished I could help him out, but I was still just a "little kid."

When Father was sick with malaria, I joined Grandpa in

caring for him. Sometimes I even took care of him myself since Grandpa was out sewing in other peoples' houses, and there was nobody else who could stay with Father. I brought him water, and every so often, wiped a rag across his forehead. The doctor promised that Father would recover, it was only a matter of time, and thanks to the durum Shimon had brought us, he might get stronger and better even faster than we'd originally thought.

My friends looked for me every morning, and I told them, "Not today, maybe tomorrow." The truth was that I preferred staying with Father and feeling that I could help out, making things a bit easier for him. I wanted him to be comfortable. When his temperature shot up, his body shivering, I wet a cloth with cold water and patted his forehead. Father slept most of the time, and I waited for him to feel better. Working in the gold mine had been too much for him, and it was lucky that he'd switched to shoemaking in the factory, so that he didn't have to spend all day digging in a tunnel, inhaling fumes. It was the second time he had been so sick since we'd arrived in Kazakhstan. I wasn't used to my strong father falling ill so suddenly and so often. But my father was the strongest person in the world, so I had no doubt that he would get better. The doctor had promised, and so had Mother and Grandpa.

Since Father had become sick, and I stayed to watch over him when everybody else was working or studying, Shifra and Sima really began to treat me like a big kid. Shifra told me, while stroking my head, that I had proven I could be trusted, and Sima smiled at me and said that not only was I being responsible and helping Father, but I also didn't cry as much as I used to, and it really looked like I was becoming mature. I smiled to myself when I heard that. If they only knew what kind of mischief I was getting into with my gang, they wouldn't be saying those things. There were days when I really wanted Father to get better already so I could go back to my shenanigans, but in the meantime, I was just trying to enjoy what I had. There were days when Father wasn't always asleep, and when he was awake, he told me stories about our village from his childhood, about Grandpa and Grandma and all my aunts and uncles, some of whose whereabouts I don't even know. Father told me these stories and sometimes a tear escaped from his eye, and I knew that even parents needed their own parents, and even when they look like grownups, they're still just kids inside.

* * *

Father got better, and I went back to wandering the streets with my gang. Once in a while, I managed to get my hands on a piece of fruit, but that was about it. Shimon continued to help the Cossacks, and they continued to give him sacks of durum in return. Mother ground the durum with special rocks that the Cossacks brought her, but I was still almost always hungry. She said that she'd give us only a small portion every day, since the sacks weren't bottomless, so it was smarter to save the rest for more difficult times, when the Cossacks weren't around.

"Ichu, winter will soon end, and the Cossacks won't need any more boots, not until the end of summer," is what Mother said. I understood what she meant, but sometimes I was just the slightest bit angry, and sometimes, I blamed God and asked when would I be full again? When would my clothes be properly patched up, that is, my own clothes and not my mother's?

Suddenly, out of nowhere, summer arrived, and the days became warmer. One day, we received some good news: The Russians had managed to ward off the Germans from Russian territory. Father heard from his factory that the Russians had taken a bunch of German soldiers as prisoners, and the rest were simply falling on the battlefield like flies. The Russians knew their own territory way better than the Germans did, which was very fortunate. I had been waiting for a long time for everything to end, so we could go back to our home in Poland.

Grandpa continued to tell us stories, refreshing our memories of the village, so that we wouldn't forget. I admit that I may have even forgotten what our house looked like, but I asked Sima to remind me, since she has a sharp memory. In great detail, she described every room in the house, and suddenly, I remembered so many things I hadn't thought about in ages—the market and the bakery, and my sweet aunt Hasya, may her memory be a blessing, who always snuck me one of those divine loaves. Grandpa became so sullen after her death, and he prayed non-stop. He was happy when we came home every night in one piece, and when we blessed the water on Fridays, since we didn't have any wine. Every Friday, Grandpa placed his hand on our heads and blessed each one of us, while Mother gazed at all of us, a serene smile on her face. I waited for that smile all week long, hoping that she wouldn't let it falter. Maybe when the damned war was over, she would smile even more.

Father said the war may be about to end, and if it does, we'll be able to go home, to Tarnobrzeg, so I can finally return to school and learn how to read and write. If the war is over by October, I'll even be able to have my bar mitzvah. I smiled at him, my heart bursting with joy at the very thought of it. Shimon didn't have his bar mitzvah either because of the war, so maybe we will be able do it together, and everything will go back to being just as it was before the war. And I hoped that Grandpa would go back to smiling and being as happy as he once was.

When Father said those words, I looked at Mother and saw the excitement etched on her face. She opened her arms wide for me to come toward her, and I did, and she hugged me. "Ichuki, a *sheine bucher*, my beloved child, almost a bar mitzvah, how time has passed so quickly," she whispered. "It seems as though you were born only yesterday." I looked at her and knew, for the first time, that the war was really going to end soon, that Father was right when he had said this whole mess we were in was only temporary.

I really believed he might be right, that maybe we would get home before my bar mitzvah, and I would read from the Torah in the grand synagogue. I imagined my entire family, even my deceased aunts and Gail's husband, who had died so long ago, and Grandma, of course, all of them looking at me proudly as Shimon and I went up to the bima to read from the Torah for the first time. I smiled, knowing that the painted whale on the ceiling wouldn't scare me anymore since now I knew it was only a painting. Then I ran to tell all my friends that the war was about to end, and they said they didn't believe a word I was saying, that "it's all nonsense, let's just go steal some plums from the market. It's the end of summer, and they're as sweet as can be.

Chapter Fifty-Four: MAYA, 2019

TEL AVIV

After dropping off the kids at summer camp and preschool, and only a few days before our trip to Holland, I listened to my recording of the meeting with Itzhak and Tzipke, thinking how crucial documenting their story was, along with the stories of all survivors. Within a decade, or two at most, there would be no survivors left, and these recordings a precious relic. I was proud of Itzhak for his fervent desire to document his life, despite his great difficulty returning to that period that he had wanted to leave behind so badly. When I had asked Tzipke if she remembered where she'd been on the day the war had ended, she'd smiled and said, "Of course I do, that's like asking if I remember where I was when Rabin was murdered or when the Twin Towers fell."

Itzhak had added, "After waiting for something for so long, suddenly it arrives, and that's a big moment."

"I remember that I was standing in the crumbling apartment we were staying in," Tzipke said. "I remember that I was extremely hungry, and it was pouring rain. I remember that my father came in and hollered, 'The war is over! The war is over!' That's what he shouted, and I ran to him and asked if it was really over. He said, 'Yes, the devils have finally lost, the Russians have won, and now we can go home.' I even remember what I had been wearing when my father entered the apartment."

Then Tzipke had asked, "Itzhak, where were you when you were told the war had ended?"

Itzhak had replied, "I was in the Zamlinka, and I heard shouting, so I went outside and saw that the streets were full of people screaming with joy, hugging each other and crying, and at first I was frightened, truly," he said with a wide smile. "People screaming everywhere, I had no idea what had happened to them, if they had gone crazy." Tzipke and I had laughed, and then Itzhak had added, "When I understood that the war was really over, I ran to look for Shimon. I marched right into his factory, but nobody was working. The wild news had reached them, too, and everyone was dancing, singing, grabbing onto each other gleefully. And when Shimon saw me, he shouted, 'Ichu, can you believe it? The war is over, Ichu, that's it! We beat those bastards!'"

Itzhak had recounted how they'd rushed back to the Zamlinka, embraced their parents, Grandpa, and their sisters, how Grandpa had recited the sheyichiyanu blessing and declared that there would be only good days moving forward. The days following the announcement were total chaos, or, as Itzhak had described it: "People suddenly didn't know their right from left; they went back to standing in line for bread, but my parents received a message from the Russians mandating them to leave Russia within a week and return to Poland."

"What did you remember of your house?" I had asked. "After all, you were young children when the war began."

Tzipke had replied that despite being only six years old when they left, she remembered it quite well, and Itzhak had said that his memory had faded, but once in a while, his mother would describe the house to them "to make sure we didn't forget that our real home was in Poland."

His mother's words had made us all emotional, and for a moment a long silence was captured on the recording, before Itzhak interjected, "It was awful, Maya, can you picture it for a second? The war ends, and you're just a kid dying to finally go home, and you're on a train with your family for weeks, then risk your life on some rickety, unsound boats, and finally you reach your village, where no house is waiting for you, not even a pair of shoes. And you get stoned by everybody in sight, so you just keep going, never again to return to the home you had so hoped would be yours again."

His words had bored into my soul on the first day we met, and had only drilled deeper since then, especially when I tried to transform them into writing. The sight of my familiar study returned me to the heat of the Israeli summer, to my home, to my children who had never known scarcity, who were enveloped by love, who lived comfortable lives and never had to imagine what it was like to suffer from the cold. That stark difference was difficult to internalize. It was even more difficult to think that there were still children who experienced want, feeling unprotected and unsheltered. I thought about Yairi and me, about the fact that we had so many of our own problems, yet were still able to provide a warm, loving home for our children, and were doing our best to work on our marriage. When I finished writing, I discovered an email from Yairi in my inbox.

My beloved Maya,

These past few months have been challenging for me, with ups and downs, both of us grappling with our own mood swings and instabilities, things which are never easy to handle. You wanted to know, so I am putting it all out here as transparently as I can, so that you know it won't ever happen again, just as I promised, and understand that I don't have anything to hide from you.

I met Ye'ela at a conference in Silicon Valley last year. She is around our age and lives in America. At the beginning, there wasn't anything between us, we just talked, like I told you, sometimes in the company of others and other times alone. Sometimes we spoke when I was at home. It was as you suspected, I wasn't speaking with Moti, but with Ye'ela. Six months ago, when I flew to Silicon Valley for a business trip, I met up with her more often. At the beginning, I felt like I was on some kind of adventure. She was simple and easygoing. Everything was just easy with her. I wanted freedom, which I only later discovered had been inside me all along. When it became more serious, I realized I needed to figure things out. The thought of breaking up our family never crossed my mind. I had really only been looking for some excitement, a spark, since I was just about to celebrate my fortieth birthday, which was horrifying to me, and you were so physically distant, and emotionally no less so.

I felt as though I couldn't share any of my interests with you. You were so absorbed with the kids and with your writing that when we finally found ourselves alone, you were tired most of the time. Slowly but surely, I began to feel lonely, rejected, and unloved, and the cherry on top was my fortieth birthday creeping up on me. I yearned for some external solution to my negative emotions. Ye'ela was right there. It could have been another woman, but she listened to me, cracked up at all my jokes, made me feel like I was some rare catch, and I became confused and fell under her spell. I know I hurt you. I have apologized many times, but I understand why my apologies haven't been received wholeheartedly. On that day when I didn't make it to the restaurant, the real reason for my absence was that Ye'ela was visiting Israel. There was no long meeting at work. I was with her, and the truth is, I didn't really want to have dinner with you since I knew our conversation would be superficial and full of lies. I'm so sorry, it was ugly and brutal of me, and you don't deserve that kind of treatment. I am truly sorry for hurting you.

Now that I've told you the entire story, I want you to know that I ended the affair quickly, with the knowledge that my relationship with Ye'ela was never authentic, at least not on my part. I wasn't authentic. I ended the affair because I knew that I wanted to be with you, to wake up with you in the morning, hear all your funny stories, and the sad ones, too, the interesting and boring ones alike. I want things to be complicated, the way they are with us. Who said that everything needs to be so simple? Simplicity is a temporary illusion. It's not real life. I want to make love to you, only with you, because only with you am I truly myself, and I hope that you'll find the strength within yourself, and the will, to come back to me, to be mine, truly mine.

I think of you and know that soon I'll go home, and you'll be there, and I'll wrap my arms around you, hoping that you might do the same, out of true love.

If you need more time, just know that I am here, waiting for you until you feel that it's right for you to come back.

I love you,
Yair

Chapter Fifty-Five: ITZHAK, 2019

JERUSALEM

For the past few weeks, Tzipke and I have been meeting once a week. She comes up to Jerusalem, and we go out to a restaurant or café, quickly making up for years of lost time. When I look at her, I still see that young girl who was my first love, and she keeps telling me that I haven't really changed. I can't do anything but laugh when I hear her saying that kind of thing, and I'm probably blushing all over. I whisper words of love to her in Yiddish, *sheindale*, my love. I gaze into her eyes, unable to believe she is by my side. We've started to discuss moving together to a different nursing home, one that will suit both of us. I have even considered the possibility of moving to Tel Aviv, which would be far away from my children, but close to my true love.

The time we have left isn't as long as the time we missed out on, but we want to spend it together. I never imagined this kind of bliss at my age. When I look at her, I think that maybe I did something good in the world after all, and that God is trying to bring a bit of happiness into my life. I pray to Him day and night, lay my tefillin, and ask for my love's good health. I really believe that He is by my side, having watched over me so many times over the course of my life, and voila, He has brought me the greatest joy.

Tzipke visited me today. We spent the morning at the Biblical Zoo and had dessert at my favorite café, Caffit. I like sitting there and looking out at the lake. Usually, I ask to be seated as close to the water as possible. Luckily, there was a free table in that spot. When we got back to my room, Maya was there. I was so happy to see her. She completed my good day. As we were putting the finishing touches on the story of my youth, she said to me, "Ichu, did you know that you're a hero? And it's a good thing that we're documenting this; otherwise, your story, along with so many others, would be lost to history." I make an effort to please her, knowing full well how right she is. Witnesses have the power to describe history as it really was, and soon our generation will be gone, and no one will be left to tell those stories. I do my part faithfully, making an effort to remember as many details as I can, despite the emotional tumult of going back to those days.

While Maya and I sat down in my room, Tzipke prepared some sweet tea, just the way I like it with a bit of lemon. After chitchatting about her kids' vacation and the Biblical Zoo, which is the most beautiful in the world, Maya asked if we'd be willing to speak a bit about our reunion in the DP camp. "If it's too much for you," she said, "tell me a bit about the day you found out the war was over." I smiled to Tzipke and told her that I'd be happy to hear her version of the story. We hadn't yet discussed that period. All I knew was that Tzipke's family had left the forests shortly before we had, but their escape route was slightly different. We met up again in the DP camp. Tzipke's family had been taken to a labor camp where they spent most of the war. After being released during the last days of the war, they followed the rumors toward the southern Russian border, settling on the shores of the Caspian Sea.

Many years after the war ended, we still rarely spoke of it. It was a difficult period that nobody wanted to relive, but we were also made to feel terribly guilty, despite the brutal years and the loss of our loved ones. For many years, the establishment did not recognize our suffering since we "weren't really Holocaust survivors if we weren't sent to the extermination camps." That sentence sliced through my heart each time anew. It was like saying that somebody who lost seven years of their life didn't have the right to complain, since other people were worse off. The death camp survivors "beat us" in the fight over who suffered more. They survived the inferno and were recognized by both the Jewish state and the German government, while we were made to feel as though we had betrayed Polish Jewry by shirking the camps. We also felt that we didn't have any right to complain about the agonizing years of suffering we went through since we "weren't really Holocaust survivors," and to top it all off, we had the chutzpah to go straight to Germany after the war. Traitors, to sum it up!

We celebrated the end of the war dancing in the streets, the feeling of euphoria buzzing all around us. People were exhausted, hungry, poor, and distraught, and suddenly we were informed that it was all over. My parents and Grandpa decided we would go back to our house, but they didn't need to wait for long, since the Russians announced that we needed to leave Russia within a week and make our way back to Poland. My parents and Grandpa couldn't have imagined there would be no house or village left from our former lives. As soon as our imminent exile from Russia was brought to our attention, we started preparing for the long trip home. Shimon said goodbye to the owner and workers of the factory where he had been employed, receiving a blessing for his journey. The factory owner commended his work. "A boy who is actually a strong man with limitless energies," is how he described him, having learned to read him well. Thanks to my brother Shimon, we had all received warm boots to get through the tough Siberian winter. I knew that he would always have my back.

We helped Mother and Father organize our few belongings and said goodbye to those we were leaving behind, knowing full well that we'd never be coming back to Kazakhstan.

Fifty-Six:
ICHU, MAY 1945

EN ROUTE BACK TO POLAND

I was so happy when the war ended, I didn't even care that I was leaving my friends behind. I said goodbye without thinking twice or crying at all. I invited them to come visit me back in Tarnobrzeg, and the next day we were off. Father said that in all the chaos, he hadn't been able to find a way for us to get out of the city, so we'd be better off starting by foot. Our neighbor Genia brought us a bit of bread for the journey. She suggested that we start walking toward the train station. "You'll see a lot of villages on the way there," she said, "and I'm sure somebody will be nice enough to take you to the train station." Father told us that the train to Poland departed from a station a few dozen kilometers away and that would be the first leg of our journey.

Mother woke me up when it was still dark out and very cold, but I opened my eyes happily. How could I not? I was about to leave that stinky place and go home! We all divided our belongings among us, and I checked that my coin was still in my pocket. It had accompanied me throughout the war years, and it still watched over me. I looked back at the Zamlinka one last time without an ounce of sadness, and we began walking. Although the Zamlinka had been a protective shelter from wind and snow, it had also been stinky and crowded. Siberia was not my favorite place, that was for sure. The sun that emerged from behind the clouds tended to be weak even in the summertime. Mother reminded us all that when we got home, we'd finally have a real summer, with the sun shining and warming our faces, chickens waddling around and vegetables growing in the garden, while Mother prepared a hot pot of cholent.

On my back, I carried a cloth sack that Grandpa had woven out of the remnants of tattered clothes "long past their heyday," Grandpa had said with a sigh. Inside the sack was a bit of food that Mother, Shifra, and Sima had prepared for the journey. Grandpa was the only one who wasn't carrying anything on his back since the walk was hard enough for him as was, but I knew that "we would help him," that he would be okay, just like my strong Grandpa always was.

When we began walking, it was really cold, even though winter was over, and it was already spring. My hands were freezing, and I stuffed them under my clothes to warm them up a little. Slowly but surely, the sun began to peek out from behind the clouds. I looked at it and smiled, sharing the anticipation of my good fortune with its rays. Father hugged me to his body and said, "Ichu, you know how proud I am of you, don't you?"

"Really?" I replied, smiling. "Why's that?"

"I'm proud of you for taking the sack on your back, for doing your best to help your brother and sisters and Grandpa, and in general, I am so proud of what has become of the sweet boy you once were." That's what Father said to me, and I knew he was in a good mood because he couldn't wipe the smile off his face, and it looked as if the prospect of going home in freedom had penetrated his bones, despite the heavy sack he carried.

The emerging sun worked its wonders in melting the ice, and we began sinking into the thawing mud that left us wet up to our ankles. Slowly, we each turned inward to focus on our own burdens, trying not to exhaust anybody else, but the mood shifted, from joy and hope to worry. We walked for long hours in silence, each one immersed in his or her own thoughts, and I noticed Father's glance shifting from side to side. Night fell, and we were all frozen down to our bones—our drenched boots only making the situation worse by adding a load of water to each step. The walk became more and more strenuous, and when it got dark and the water that had been melted by the sun froze again, our shoes stuck to the ice, and the walk became even more difficult. Father instructed us to keep going, saying that if we stopped, we'd freeze: "Just a bit longer, soon someone will come by and give us a ride," he said. But there was nothing and nobody around us, not a village or a single soul to whom we could cry for help.

I saw that Grandpa was having a hard time walking. Mother looked worried, Shimon kept cursing under his breath, and Sima and Shifra didn't dare laugh at his expletives. Sure, we might've survived the war up until now—at least most of us, minus Grandma and our aunts and Aunt Gail's husband—but if some miracle didn't happen, we might freeze to death on this cursed path that seemed to have no end. We didn't stop walking even though we were hungry and cold, and Father said, "Just you wait, God watched over us all these years; He's watching over us today, too," which strengthened us, so we kept walking, a bit slower, dragging one foot after the other, looking down at the ground, doing our best to avoid any deep pits.

We forged ahead like that until it was almost completely dark.

All of a sudden, I saw Father and Shimon running like madmen. At first, I was frightened, seeing that Mother didn't understand why and where they were going, watching her shout at them to slow down, to watch out for the pits, afraid that if one of them fell, nobody would be able to save them from the swampy mud; but they kept on running. From far away, we heard them shouting in Russian, and then we noticed a faraway carriage, and we all began walking faster; even Grandpa's feet pretty much sprouted wings as he sped up to my pace, and I saw Father and Shimon arriving with the carriage on the verge of fainting.

The prayers Grandpa Eli recited all day long had finally borne fruit. The carriage driver stared at us, struggling to understand where we had come from. He even got off the carriage and helped lift us up. He promised to take us to the village since, "somebody there will host you," and that's what happened. In the late evening, we knocked on the door of one of the village houses that still had a light in its window. A tired peasant woman, no less surprised than the driver to be greeted by a crowd of emaciated travelers, opened the door. "Christus, bozhe moi," she murmured. "Where did you come from, what are you doing here?" Mother explained that we had departed from Djalimbrad and were on our way home to Poland, "but we didn't find a way out of the city, since the trains are on strike."

"Come, come in." I studied the woman's face and etched it in my mind, knowing now what angels looked like. The peasant woman warmed some water on the stove and helped us take off our boots, which were soaked in slush. She touched my feet and asked if I could feel anything. I nodded. Smiling, she said, "You've been saved, my boy." I was happy that was the case, and I began to wonder what would have happened if my foot had really frozen. How would I be able to jump and run? I didn't think about it for too long, since the peasant woman brought us a bit of bread and cream, and then we all huddled near the stove and fell asleep.

In the morning, we said goodbye to the woman and continued our walk to the train station. There was still a long, arduous way to go, but we were lucky it wasn't raining. On the way, we saw other families on the move, which made our own walk a bit easier. I knew that the walk was hardest on Grandpa Eli, so I didn't dare complain. If an old man like him could walk so heroically, I could be a hero, too.

On the way, we stopped to eat something and have a sip of water, but not for too long, knowing that we needed to arrive before nightfall. As the sun was setting, we suddenly saw the train station in the distance, and we all smiled. "That's it, we're leaving Russia and going home to Tarnobrzeg." The truth was that I couldn't even recall at that point what our house looked like, but I did remember the room that I had shared with my brother, the smells of Shabbat dinner, and even the backyard in which we'd played together with the neighbor's kids. Then suddenly I realized I didn't know whether they'd come back; I really hoped so, and I thought about Tzipke, who was almost my age, just as mischievous as me, and as brave as a boy; but then Shimon said to me, "Ichu, stop dreaming, you almost fell into a pit, watch where you're going." I looked back and saw that I'd dodged a huge pit, so I stopped thinking about our house and village and the rest of the kids. I was tired and hungry and all I wanted to do was sit.

Chapter Fifty-Seven: MAYA, 2019

TEL AVIV

That night, I held Yairi close to me. We both cried and kissed and then hugged each other tighter and cried some more. Luckily, the kids were too glued to the T.V. to catch the drama unfolding before their eyes. I told Yairi that I forgave him, truly and fully, that I was grateful for his letter, and only sorry that I hadn't expressed what I needed to hear from him earlier on. I promised to be his friend, just as I had promised when we'd said our vows, and he vowed that we'd continue to grow together after everything we'd been through, until one day we'd wake up and realize how tall we'd become. I laughed in between tears, and then we went to tell the kids we were all going to Holland the following week.

The older kids jumped for joy, while Gali asked if we were taking the bus. We said there would definitely be a bus involved, maybe also a train, and if we got lucky, we'd fly in a plane, too. "Yay!", she shouted, and joined the celebration. We spent the next days going over our itinerary with the kids, and they were thrilled.

When the morning of the trip was finally upon us, we woke up the children before dawn. They seemed to have barely slept from all the excitement. Gali had fallen asleep late, after three stories and two songs; Avishay had decided to sleep in his flight outfit; and Dana had camped out in Avishay's room, the two of them talking and giggling in hushed tones until we declared that "whoever doesn't go to sleep immediately will sleep at Grandma Doris' instead of coming to Holland." They were immediately quiet and conked out soon afterward. Yair and I finished packing everyone's suitcases, and we fell asleep for a few hours.

We didn't hear the alarm clock ring, but luckily Gali crawled into our bed for her usual nightly snuggle half an hour after we were supposed to wake up, which transformed our plans for a speedy egress into a speed-of-light egress. We pulled the kids out of bed, ordered another cab, since the first one was already long gone, grabbed our suitcases and headed out, after making sure we hadn't misplaced any of the passports or medicines. "Everything else we can buy in Holland," we assured ourselves. "We always forget something important, but we're all here, two parents and three kids, which is the most important," Yairi joked loudly; and I joined his laughter.

We waited outside for a few minutes, which dragged on like hours in Tel Aviv's sultry heat. August was a tough month, unforgiving day and night. The heat and humidity were stubborn, holding on until their last hurrah, never easing in their intensity. When the taxi arrived, we sighed with relief; there was still a chance we'd make the flight. Yair helped the driver load the suitcases into the trunk, while we sat in the back. The driver, detecting our distress, did his best to get to the airport as fast as he could; when we arrived, we were the last ones to get on the plane.

Gali threw up as the plane took off, the grand finale to a crying session that had erupted just before. After I changed her clothes and cleaned us both off, she quickly fell asleep in my arms. Dana and Avishay took out the workbooks and iPad we'd brought along for them and announced that they were hungry. I rummaged through my bag for the sandwiches Yairi had prepared for them the night before and handed one to each. Looking content, Avishay said that "flying was the most fun ever, except for when Gali threw up and made everything smell bad." Dana smiled and said, "It is stinky, isn't it?" as she pinched her nose with her thumb and index finger. I checked my clothes again to see if I had missed a spot of vomit, finding one on my pants. I had turned out to be the source of the stench. I asked Yair to take Gali while I tried to clean myself off again. Luckily, I always pack an extra set of clothing when we fly, just in case the suitcases don't arrive. After I realized that nothing else would do the trick, I went to the bathroom and changed clothes. When I came out, I found my happy-go-lucky buddies absorbed in a Disney move, Yair napping, and Gali sleeping deeply. I gazed at my family and a wave of warmth and gratitude washed over me.

Chapter Fifty-Eight: ITZHAK, MAY 1945

EN ROUTE BACK TO POLAND

The journey to Poland lasted for weeks on end, during which we mostly slept in train stations with other refugees. As long as we were within Russian territory, the Russians provided us with ration slips. It was not an easy trip, but I was reassured by the prospect of returning home, to the village we had left six years earlier, to our quaint little house, our synagogue, our local market, and daily routine. Along the way, rumors of pogroms in Poland against Jews returning to their homes reached our ears. Father said he hoped they were only rumors, and Mother said, "The Poles have always been anti-Semites, nothing they do will surprise me." But I knew they were both anticipating the moment they'd see their brothers and sisters again, their nieces, nephews, cousins, and the entire extended family from whom they'd been separated since the beginning of the war.

The rumors of what had happened to the Jews reached us when we were on the border between Russia and Poland. Mother burst into tears, and Grandpa prayed for their souls. Father didn't know which of his family members had survived the war; as more information became available, he discovered that only two of his brothers were still alive. Besides that, I remember that we looked terrible. Our clothes were ragged, we were thin, and us children didn't look even close to our real ages. I had just celebrated my thirteenth birthday but could easily have been mistaken for a little boy.

I remember thinking for a long time about my bar mitzvah, wondering when I'd be able to celebrate that important day. When I scan my memory for mental images from that journey, I am reminded of the faces of each of my family members when we got off the train at the first stop after crossing the Polish border. The station was in Szczecin, and the only person waiting for us was our neighbor Mordechai, who had left behind his family, leaving his daughter in my father's care, and had now come to receive us warmly. After a series of emotional hugs, Mordechai thanked my father and admitted that he had made a mistake in abandoning his family. My father replied, "Not to worry, sometimes even the wisest among us make mistakes."

That's the kind of person my father was, strong and merciful like a lion, and Mordechai had known that he could entrust him with his family when he'd departed on his crazy journey. Only God knows how he managed to get out of there alive. But sometimes miracles happen, other times misfortune befalls us, and in that period, I tried to stay positive and see only the good. Maybe it was a product of my young age, but I'm not so sure. One of the things that held us together back then, and that still keeps my spirit intact today, is optimism—even in the depths of the treacherous unknown, there always has to be at least one good thing to hold on to.

From the train station, we went to the apartment my aunt Gail was staying in with her two daughters, Feichu and Hichu. Noah and Rachel were there, too. It was a moment of overwhelming joy mixed with inconsolable sorrow as we realized that most of our other family members were gone forever. When I travel through my mind back to our journey home, I am often left breathless. How painfully astonishing was the fact that our suffering was not yet over. Not only had we been banished from our homes, considered lucky to have made it out alive, and endured the war with many losses and countless difficulties, we weren't even sure we'd have somewhere to return to. At the end of it all, we found ourselves continuing by train to the refugee camp in Heidenheim, Germany, which was a gathering place for many refugees at the time.

Chapter Fifty-Nine: ICHU, SEPTEMBER 1945

POLAND

It was a long journey back from Russia. We spent days, nights, weeks on trains, and wherever the tracks had been demolished by bombs, we had to go by foot. And still the Polish border was nowhere in sight. I always kept my eyes out for a sign of Tzipke and her family, praying with all my might that they were still alive. I told Mother that not knowing what had happened to the Voronski family was scary, but Mother said she trusted that Tzipke's father had taken care of them as best he could, and they were probably okay. "Ichu, don't worry so much," she said, "life is full of surprises. Maybe they're not always the surprises we hope for, but sometimes they end up being better than we could have imagined." I admit that at that point, all I could say to my mother was that I really hoped she was right, but I wasn't convinced anymore; I had discovered that mothers don't always know everything, and neither do fathers. I sat quietly, channeling all my thoughts toward Tzipke, hoping that if I concentrated hard enough, she would appear in front of me. But that didn't work, either.

Father insisted that we try to go back to Tarnobrzeg, while Grandpa said that it was a stupid, dangerous idea, but that if it was so important to Father, we could see if there was any chance of getting off at the closest train station and try going home—if home even existed anymore. Grandpa said those words with a sharp bitterness—a tone I had learned to recognize in his voice since Aunt Hasya's death. He seemed unsettled, while trying to maintain a sense of calm for our collective welfare. We rode for a few more hours on one train, then hopped onto another, and by evening, we'd arrived at the closest train station to Tarnobrzeg. From the train, the widespread damage from the bombing was visible, adding to our doubts that we still had a home to which we would return.

A few Jewish families we'd known before the war joined us on our way back to the village. To my dismay, Tzipke's family wasn't among them, but at least there were others. I remembered that one of them had been a family of eight children, but I noticed that only three, who were already teenagers, were present. I didn't dare ask what had happened to the rest. I could guess without too much trouble. It turned out that they had arrived from the far border between China and Russia, making it all the way back to Poland. When the war had ended, the Russians had placed them on the first train back, and since then, they had been on the road home for several weeks, approximately the same amount of time as us. We were excited to have them with us. I was reminded of Shmulik, who had been the same age as me. He wasn't with them, and I could only imagine what had become of that smiley kid with the mischievous eyes, who had been in the same *cheder* as me as a kid, receiving far more slaps on the wrist from the rabbi than I had, unable to stay quiet even when the rabbi slapped him over and over again. The children who had made it out alive were just as thin as we were. They had one daughter who I didn't remember, but who looked to be around five or six at that point, and two more boys around Shifra and Shimon's age. I didn't remember most of the other families who were with us. It was hard to recognize them. They were emaciated and had grown and changed, just as I had. I assumed that I looked just as strange to them as they did to me.

When we were about to get off the train, I heard screams from outside. "Are there any more Jews still alive?"

Some Poles had seen the Jews getting off the trains, making their way home. They shouted aggressively, and at first, I thought they were happy shouts, making me feel even more certain that I'd finally get to sleep in my own warm bed that night, but then I heard screams of agony. Father ordered us to stay where we were. I looked outside and saw Mordechai Podolski, a man from our village, still wearing his Anders Army uniform.[2] He was injured, his face drenched in blood. I didn't recognize the uniform, but Grandpa told me that he had fought the Nazis alongside the British. Mother urged us not to move, while Father stood up to see how he could help. Gripping his arm, Mother said, "Israel, you are not getting off right now. We are not getting off." She shot him a menacing look, and I knew that Father wouldn't dare budge. I was happy that Mother's resourcefulness kept us safe. Father knew not to get on her bad side, so he just stood there with a helpless look on his face. The train rumbled onward with us still on it.

---

[2] The Anders Army was named after its Polish commander, general Władysław Anders. The name refers to the Eastern Polish Army or the Polish armed force in the Soviet Union, a Polish armed force loyal to the Polish government-in-exile in London, founded in the Soviet Union during World War II.

It turned out that the Polish train workers, hearing that some Jews had indeed survived, at least a few of them, had pelted those who dared return with rocks. Mordechai's wife, whom Mordechai hadn't seen since the beginning of the war, had been hit by one such rock. Brandishing a pistol, Mordechai shouted at the Poles, "Stop throwing rocks immediately, or I'll shoot and kill you all." I saw Mordechai's wife, blood dripping down her face as she lay on the ground and couldn't figure out if she was dead or alive. All I knew was that she had traveled all the way from Russia to meet her husband, and instead, she seemed to have met her death.

Mother tried to cover my eyes and instructed my sisters not to look, but it didn't change anything. We were all aghast at the horror unfolding before us, at the same time that we were thankful for having been saved once again, this time from the pogroms. After a few minutes of silence, I asked Father, "Where are we going now?" having realized that a warm bed was not in store for me that night. Father said that we could no longer go home, maybe one day in the future, but that he knew of a place in Germany that was taking in Jews, giving them food and shelter. Mordechai got back on the train and said there was no point in getting off. "We're going to Germany, to the part that's been occupied by the Americans. They'll take care of us."

Father had helped Mordechai Podolski lift his wife's body onto the train, and we buried it at the next station where we weren't pelted with rocks. Then we got on a different train that took us to the Czech border where we met local smugglers who remembered what Mordechai had done for them, and as a result, they smuggled us into Germany. On the way there, we met Zionist activists, who spoke in praise of the "Jewish state of Palestine." Father said quietly that he thought we should continue to Palestine from Germany since, "we might be respected there, and nobody will call us names anymore just because we are Jews."

* * *

With the help of Mordechai's friends, we arrived in Ostrava, Czechoslovakia, late at night, and Mother said we could finally relax. We had successfully passed the most difficult border crossings, the only one remaining being the German border, which was simpler. We spent the night under the stars. It was hot outside, and we might have been mistaken for a bunch of friends on a summer camping trip, rather than refugees on the final leg of a years-long voyage for survival. We were all shadows of our former selves. When I got up, Father, Shimon, and Grandpa were already praying *shaharit* with the rest of the men, while the women gathered the few belongings we'd brought with us all the way from Russia.

My shoes were so tattered that at times I felt I was walking barefoot; but the smells of summer and the end of the war made me happy, and I told Sima that I knew today was going to be a good day, since we would be arriving at the camp in Heidenheim in Germany.

The Czech men Mordechai had brought along to help us promised that in Czechoslovakia, no one would throw rocks at us because we were Jews. We had nothing to worry about. So, we didn't worry; we were just happy to have left Poland, and I was beginning to understand that we'd never go back there.

Who wanted to live with a bunch of anti-Semites, anyway? But Mother said they weren't all like that, that there would always be those who hated Jews, or black people, or somebody else. After thinking about it a bit, I decided I would never hate anybody because of their origin, and I even told Mother my thoughts, to which she replied, "Ichu, you know, I see you've come out of this war with some important wisdom, and I am proud of you. You should always choose compassion and love over everything else." I looked at my mother, who was dressed in rags, thin as a leaf, her face wrinkled and tired, and I told her that I loved her the most in the entire world.

We kept on walking together quietly for a few hours, until we reached a small house in a nearby village, where two smugglers, who Mordechai knew from the Anders Army, lived. Suddenly, it seemed like the whole world was friends with our friend. I stood silently as they explained how to drive the mule-drawn carriage. We got on and rode for a few hours until we arrived at the train station where we got off. The smugglers said that they'd leave us there and told us to take a train into the part of Germany that was under American control. That was what they said, although it seemed strange to me to intentionally ride into the heart of the Nazi homeland, even if it had been conquered. I cursed the Nazis, and Father didn't say a word. He seemed to agree with me. We got on the train heading to Germany, and the next day we arrived at the DP camp in Heidenheim.

Chapter Sixty: MAYA, 2019

AMSTERDAM, HOLLAND

When we landed in Amsterdam, it was already afternoon. We rushed to pick up the suitcases, the stroller, and of course, the children. Gali sat in the stroller, and we walked toward the metro. "Only a few stops, that's all," is what Yairi said to me, and I repeated his words to the children, who were sandwiched between the hundreds of people swarming the station. As we descended the elevator to the train, it suddenly dawned upon Avishay that he was "extremely hungry," and Dana muttered through gritted teeth, "I need to pee, now!" I stared at my children, praying for patience to float down on me from the sky.

The screech of the incoming train was deafening. It seemed as though the world's entire population had arrived at this same spot in Amsterdam to board the train together. "We need to take Dana to the bathroom," I told Yairi, who said that he would take her, but we shouldn't move from our spots because otherwise he wouldn't be able to find us. So, we stood there, Gali, Avishay, and I, waiting in the middle of the crowded platform, with three suitcases, backpacks, and a half-eaten sandwich that I'd taken out of my bag—the last one left. As I stood there absorbing my surroundings, I couldn't help but think of little Ichu in his own crowded train stations, hungry, carrying little in his luggage, dressed in rags, unlike my own children, who didn't lack a thing. When I stood there, I tried to imagine their long ride home to Poland, which hadn't ended in a warm home, but in a DP camp. Yet again, he had been pushed away, forced into instability, unable to guess where he'd turn up next and when.

Avishay brought me back to Earth, shaking me and asking, "Where are Aba and Dana? We've been standing here forever. Do you think they got lost?"

I hadn't thought of the possibility that Yairi might not find us. Then I realized that we were in the Earth's underbelly, without any cell service, and I began to worry. How would I find them in this commotion? Luckily, Gali thought we were playing some sort of game of hide-and-seek, and that we'd soon find Dana and Aba, reminding me that little kids always come up with the most wonderfully simple solutions to difficult problems. After a few moments of panic, I suddenly saw Dana running to us, Yairi smiling behind her, waving his arms in the air sheepishly. When they made it back to us, he said that the restrooms had been a ways away, and as a result, he'd totally gotten lost. Gali laughed and said, "Aba and Dana found us," and Avishay groaned that they had won the game. Together, we continued toward the correct platform then got on the metro that took us to the city center, but the feeling of being in a new, unfamiliar place with my family members, compared to the Ozer family's return home, wouldn't leave my mind. I couldn't conceive how people had survived the war for so many years, only to be unable to return to their homes, forced to spend a few more years in a DP camp and then embarked for Israel, a country rising from the dust, where they would begin a new life from scratch, unwilling to let their darkest memories and their lost loved ones hold them back, difficult as it may be. How did people start over after enduring that kind of suffering? The questions coursed through my mind, and Yairi, who sensed that I was being too quiet, asked if everything was okay. I stroked his kind face and said, "Better than okay. You're here, the kids are here, and we're on vacation. There's nothing better in the entire world."

Chapter Sixty-One: ICHU, NOVEMBER 1945

GERMANY, DISPLACED PERSONS CAMP

Tzipke's family arrived at the DP camp before us. We arrived at dusk. Our day had begun before sunrise, after crossing yet another border and entering the American zone, which was no easy feat. I was tired, oh so tired; I yearned to find a place I could call home, somewhere I could live for today and tomorrow, maybe even a year or two—something a little more stable.

I was hungry and tired, and when we entered the camp gates, American soldiers led us to a house at the edge of the street. I noticed a girl, or more precisely, a teenager, staring at us near the house toward which we were being led by the American soldiers. As we got closer, I noticed something about her: She had huge, mesmerizing blue eyes, and a gaze that was all too familiar. Could it be Tzipke? I didn't dare hope that it was really her, but she called out, "The Ozer family! The Ozer family! Ichu, Sima, Shifra, Shimon!" She ran toward us and we toward her, falling into each other's arms in an enveloping embrace.

It really was Tzipke, who led us to another house at the edge of the block, where her mother, father, and two brothers waited. It appeared that we would be neighbors again, just as we had been at home. From that day on, we played together every day, and swore never to part again. When the time came, we vowed to get married.

Chapter Sixty-Two: ICHU, OCTOBER 1946

Germany, Displaced Persons Camp

I will never forget this happy day. A year after arriving at the DP camp, Grandpa decided that I'd start preparing for my bar mitzvah since I was almost fifteen years old, after all. Since then, I've been studying very seriously in school—not that I've forgotten how to fool around and be a kid, of course. Finally, today I will read from the Torah. Grandpa has been preparing me for this momentous occasion for weeks on end, and luckily, the Hebrew classes at the camp's makeshift school are no joke. I am learning to read in the Holy tongue, but I am also learning the Hebrew of today, and discovering many words from the Torah that are used now. In the village, the language of the Torah was considered Holy; but after the war the world turned upside down, and the secular and the Holy began mixing together, which was a little confusing but also very exciting. To think that in ancient times people spoke the language I was learning to speak was both strange and fascinating.

From time to time, when we got really bored, Tzipke and I would speak in Hebrew, rolling around with laughter because it sounded ridiculous to speak all those languages together—Hebrew, Yiddish, Polish, Russian, even some German and English. Over those many years, we needed to get by in all sorts of languages, even sign language for when we met kids whose language we didn't know the first thing about, which, to be honest, happened a bunch of times. The languages have all gotten mixed up. Sometimes we started a sentence in Hebrew, moved on to Yiddish, which is our native language, the language everybody spoke in the village—that is, that the Jews spoke in the village. From there we found ourselves drifting into other languages, jumbling the words and creating our own sort of international tongue.

Grandpa sewed a new suit for me, especially for my bar mitzvah. It made me look like a man. That's what Mother said when she saw me in it. Grandpa said he felt lucky that I agreed to wear a suit made by him, that I didn't insist on wearing torn pants like those worn by people who came from Palestine. Why would I, when I was so proud to wear something that Grandpa Eli sewed especially for my special day? I was happy to have those hemmed pants, so that I when I grew taller, they would grow with me, vertically and horizontally—that's what Grandpa said with a wide smile on his face. The truth was that from the moment he began sewing the suit until the moment he finished, Grandpa said I must've grown in both directions, and I believed him. I ate so much after our arrival that I thought I might very well be a giant in no time.

On that morning, like every other morning, we rose at the crack of dawn, and Grandpa helped me lay tefillin in the synagogue. Up until then, I'd practiced using Grandpa's or my father's, but that day I laid my own for the first time. Grandpa bought them especially for me. I don't know how much they cost, but I'm pretty sure it was a lot of money.

Grandpa said not to ask too many questions, so I thanked him and gave him a hug. I knew that I would keep them safe until the day I died. Tears welled up in Grandpa's and Father's eyes, and even Shimon had to hide his own when he saw my new tefillin wrapped along my arm.

Shimon had also received tefillin from Grandpa when he read from the Torah soon after we got to Heidenheim. Now we stood in the synagogue, and the men all looked at me with proud disbelief as I read. I didn't make even one mistake. Grandpa and Father stood on either side of me, their hands on my shoulder, and I was so happy they were both with me, I'll never forget it. Not to mention Shimon and my uncles, Tzipke's brothers and her father, and all the other people there, some who were also from my village and had known me since the day I was born. Mother made herring to celebrate in the evening.

In my pocket was the coin that had accompanied me every second of the day since leaving Tarnobrzeg. Like the tefillin, the coin would always be with me, to remind me of the long, taxing journey I'd endured. I did my best to keep it safe, just as I did my best to keep Mother, Father, my sisters, and Grandpa safe, and Tzipke, my dear friend, who I will marry when the time comes. That's what we agreed on as small children, and that's what we decided again when we met in the camp, just like a Hanukkah miracle.

Chapter Sixty-Three: ITZHAK, 2019

TEL AVIV

In my old age, I experienced a rebirth of sorts. The great miracle that occurred cannot be taken for granted. My entire life had passed before my eyes so quickly, and just as I had lost my eyesight, just as I had almost entirely lost my hearing, so too had I lost my hope to ever meet the lost love of my youth again. I think about the long years in which we each lived separate lives, neither of us able to imagine that the memory of the other remained so vivid. In my wildest dreams, I couldn't imagine that I was still tucked tightly away in the heart of the love of my youth, just as she had stayed in mine; and of course, I had had no way of knowing if she was even alive, or whether she still lived in a faraway land. The thought of her being in Israel and living only an hour's drive from me never crossed my mind. And here we were now, a pair of practically ancient pensioners, leaning on each other for support, exploring the Tel Aviv streets like teenagers.

We stop on the side of the road and sit on a green bench, its paint peeling, gazing out at the leafy trees along the boulevard that connects Jaffa to the Bima theater. Yesterday, we even saw a play in Yiddish, our childhood tongue.

In this mamaloschen, I whisper love poems in her ear, and

she squeezes my hand, her eyes telling me all I need to know about her heart's desire. I don't need her to return any of my rhetoric, knowing full well that her heart is surging with love for me. Love becomes an independent force after a certain period of time. That's how I have come to understand our dance. Love has its language, its players, its aura, and it provides warmth, goodness, and a sense of home, because love is a home—a familiar, beloved, sturdy home—that one can always return to. Sometimes it can also be an insufferable pain, a blow from which we barely recover. I've experienced both versions, but I have also been blessed with the love of my youth coming back to me. I have no intention of ever letting her go ever again.

I savor every second we spend together, and sometimes, I find myself missing my beloved Tzipke even when her palm is enclosed in mine. We sit on the bench for a long time, sometimes in silence, and at times, one of us excitedly remembers something we forgot to tell the other, and we dive into a long conversation. At other times, we speak about our children, about Tzipke's grandchildren, my grandchildren, and even about my great grandchildren—I have two of them, both born last year. Sitting on the bench on the side of the road, we observe the sky and the trees, the flowers and the people strolling along the boulevard. We notice two fathers, and in between them, a small child; Tzipke smiles at them and I at her, knowing she's thinking what I'm thinking, that love has no boundaries. She's open to everything, like a field in bloom, a limitless sea, understanding that only other peoples' minds feign the limits of love. "Come, Tzipke," I whisper, "let's go back to my room and make love." Tzipke smiles at me and blushes; when I rise, she links her arm into mine, and we take slow steps together toward the nursing home.

I moved into Tzipke's nursing home two weeks ago. A room had opened up not far from hers, and since then we have been catching up on those lost years, making the most with what we have left. I gaze into her eyes and find the same mischievous look she always had. Some things never change. When we met in the DP camp, we were both survivors. Tzipke was with her family, of which only half remained, and I was with mine, at least what was left of it. When I saw her that first time, I recognized her only because of those mischievous eyes. It was always the same look, even when she was a little girl; that part of her never changed. In the DP camp, we very quickly became inseparable. Everywhere Tzipke went, I went after her, and vice versa. If we had been old enough, it's safe to say we would have gotten married, but we were still children. We were good children, albeit rowdy, getting into all sorts of unbelievable mischief, the kind that only children who have gone through hell and back can create.

Tzipke and I—we had both wanted to conquer the world, to make up for the childhood we'd missed out on. We both studied at the makeshift school, built hastily from the ground up, to acquire a rudimentary knowledge of the Hebrew language; we studied math and the history of the Jewish people and even some geography. It was there that we both learned for the first time what Zionism was. I remember soaking up every fact I was given, like a dry sponge thirsty for water. I wanted so badly to learn about the world around me, and at the same time, I felt a great urge to somehow compensate for the childhood that had been cruelly robbed from me.

I didn't always know my limits. I wasn't exactly a boy, more of a grown-up boy, who had learned through life experiences that resilience was the key to survival. My parents and Grandpa Eli were the heroes of my childhood; thanks to them, my brother and I remained alive and survived the war. Danger was not a concept we understood any longer. After school, Tzipke and I would put on the skates we'd been given and skate around the wet streets, hanging on to passing cars for a speedy thrill. More than once, the drivers stopped in frustration and shouted at us, "You crazy kids! What do you think you're doing?" I would give Tzipke my hand, and we'd both skate away from them to safety, laughing like maniacs, waiting for our breath to steady before we headed home.

After accompanying Tzipke to their small house, which was right next to ours at the edge of the camp, I'd go back home to devour the warm meal Mother had prepared, as if I had never seen food before and as if I might not see another morsel again. Mother was happy seeing me eat such large portions, saying, "Ichu, the war is over, there'll be enough left over for dinner, too." She would say those words with a wide smile, and we both knew what she meant; I, too, hoped that we wouldn't go hungry ever again. And with the lust for life I had at that moment, I didn't think of anything beyond the present moment, and that was that.

Chapter Sixty-Four: MAYA, 2019

Amsterdam, Holland

We woke up to rain-soaked streets, but the morning sun worked its magic, and soon enough, we all had smiles on our faces. Venturing out into the narrow streets, we ate breakfast at a small café then rented bikes and continued toward the park. Avishay rode his own bike, while Yairi rented a tandem one to ride with Dana. Gali sat in a kid's seat attached to my bike, and that's how we set out. On the way, we stopped at a small supermarket for water, bread, cheese, and an assortment of fruits. The plan was to eat our picnic lunch in the park.

The kids' cheerful demeanors rubbed off on me. I hadn't ridden a bike in a long time, let alone for such a stretch with my entire family. The kids didn't even complain, not even Gali, who I knew wasn't having the easiest time of it in her seat. By the time we stopped for lunch, we were already beat. I spread the disposable tablecloth from the supermarket out on the grass, and we placed our food and drinks on top of it. Within minutes, the stock was ransacked, and all that was left of the previous moment were four tired people and an energetic little girl. Avishay laughed and said that Gali needed to learn how to ride a bike, so we wouldn't have to entertain her when we were pooped, and we all laughed. Only Gali pouted, brightening when I asked if she wanted to go look for the playground from Google Maps. We pedaled for a few more minutes until we got to the playground, where we spent a few hours until it was time to return the bikes.

Over the next few days, we traipsed through the city, ending each day in the massive park near our hotel, engaging the kids in various activities. After the kids had gone to sleep, Yairi and I snuck in some quiet time for ourselves, watching the kids sleeping in the other room, enjoying the rare silence around us, Holland's unique charm, and each other's company. It appeared our relationship was beginning to mend. The vacation reminded me what I hadn't really needed reminding of—I had married this man who was only becoming more remarkable as the years passed. He was my best friend; I felt more at home with him than I felt with anybody else, such that I didn't even think about the book I was struggling to finish because of my unwillingness to let go of the characters—whether real or fictional—who I longed to hold onto for a bit longer. Although this book had captured all my compassion, I still didn't feel that the characters had revealed all that they needed to reveal. But stepping back a bit was good for me because it let me miss them. Toward the end, my writing was sharpened, providing me with relief and satisfaction and making me appreciate our oh-so-needed trip even more. It had truly been an exhausting, upside-down year.

On our last day in Holland, we rose early in the morning and packed our bags, making sure we weren't forgetting anything or anyone, and headed for the park. Afterward, we drove for a few hours, stopping to stock up on sandwiches and snacks for the road, then continued quietly toward the airport, from which we flew home. Back in Israel, we were greeted by a sticky heat, so typical for August, which seemed to never end, but I didn't care. The kids said, "Gross, so humid, disgusting," and Yairi said that it was the perfect weather for the beach, and that Grandma Judith had promised that the jellyfish were all gone, and after work, he'd take them all to the beach. I thought how much I had missed my private corner at home, my computer, my desk, daily routine, and I told Yairi that the beach sounded like a great idea.

Chapter Sixty-Five: ITZHAK, 2019

TEL AVIV

The days and nights pass us by with boundless euphoria. I waited a whole lifetime to feel this way, but I knew it had been worth the wait the day I laid eyes on Tzipke again. One is born into a certain family at a certain point in history, navigating life to the best of one's abilities. There are days when life flows like a pleasant stream, and others, when you can't see the light at the end of the dark tunnel in which you are trapped.

I've tasted some of everything in my life. I was born in a small village in eastern Poland to a warm, loving family, and then a war began, one that shaped my life in more ways than I can describe. After these eighty-seven years of life, my nightmares still hound me, and I can easily go overboard with my morning hunger, asking myself if I will ever be truly satiated—not only physically, but also mentally.

And voila, I arrived in the Holy Land, the asylum for all Jewish people, where I thought my hardships would be over. But they continued, in the form of conflicts between nations, battles for survival, and wars within relationships and families, all of which God sees from above and is more than familiar with. But here, in my final days, I have been blessed with tranquility and the beauty of true love. And as a result, my youth has returned to me, the way a man returns to his God, or to his land, perhaps even without knowing what it looks like or how it will make him feel.

In the morning, I wake up to the song of birds chirping outside my window, knowing that my love is waiting for me in her room. I will rise, wash my face, lay the tefillin I received from my beloved Grandpa Eli, may his memory be a blessing; then I'll get dressed and greet the love of my youth with a "Good morning" and a bundle of kisses. Together, we'll go to the dining room and drink our coffee. She'll smile and ask me how I slept, and I'll reply that I spent the night missing her. She'll blush, put her hand in mine, look into my eyes and tell me that she feels exactly the same.

When we finish our breakfast, we'll go out into the fresh air, to the small park outside our nursing home. On some days, we'll stroll along the pretty boulevard, and other days, we'll take a taxi to the beach in the afternoon. With the sunset performing for us in the center of the sky, Tzipke will rest her head on my shoulder, and I'll whisper words of love in her ear, "*Sheindele, meidale*," my love. Sometimes, we'll take a dip in the sea, then sit and watch the water and the people playing matkot in the sand, click clack click clack, until the sun goes down and disappears. For a moment, I'll experience a slight panic, the kind that hits me whenever I see a sunset—can anybody really guarantee that the sun will rise the next day? Tzipke will know that's what I'm thinking about, having told her this silly thought many times, and she'll squeeze my hand and remind me that the sun always returns the next day. Night exists, too, and what's important is that we're together. On Saturday, the kids will come, her grandchildren, my grandchildren, my two tiny great-grandchildren. We'll sit in the café near the nursing home and eat lunch together. The kids will play, and the adults will chat; when we part ways—only "until next week," that's what they promise—we'll walk slowly to my one and only Tzipke's room. We'll lie down together for an afternoon nap, embracing one another, and, just like every Saturday, I'll know that I have made it home.

Chapter Sixty-Six: MAYA, 2019

TEL AVIV

Ichu's story was winding down. In the meantime, the new school year had begun. Avishay was starting sixth grade, his final year of elementary school. On the first day of school, I couldn't help but feel proud as my boy walked through the school gates. He's the kind of kid who always notices when other kids are struggling and offers to help out. This time, it was a new kid who had just arrived from the United States and who spoke very little Hebrew. Avishay offered to sit next to him in class. His teacher said they got along instantly, and that Avishay had set a good example for the rest of the class.

Dana is starting third grade. Her teacher is known to be amazing, and all the parents want their kids to be in her class. Anat was Avishay's teacher back in the day, and she also taught Dana last year, and now she would keep moving up with them. Dana sits next to Lihi, her friend since kindergarten. The two girls have playdates at least twice a week after school, once at our place, and once at Lihi's. Gali is in her final year of preschool. Lior's son, Matan, is at a different school, which means I no longer see his handsome father Lior in the morning or at pick-up time.

A few weeks ago, Ichu moved into Tzipke's nursing home. Whenever I meet him, those two lovebirds prove that age is just a number. Some people are young at heart, others are old souls, and most people exist somewhere in between, seeking balance.

During my previous visits to Itzhak and Tzipke's nursing home, they told me about the time they spent in Heidenheim, and I learned about the Zionist movement that had sparked their initial interest in Israel. After the long war years, their families met again, and the love between the two youths was rekindled. This time, it wasn't a friendship between kids, but two teenagers making up for their lost youth and other losses, recreating whatever childhood they could still salvage, in all its beauty and joy. The families were neighbors again, exactly as they had been before the war, and the shared experiences in Heidenheim extended to their families as well.

The wave of Zionism that rippled through the camp sparked a desire in the young people to move to a country in its infancy. Shimon was the first to make Aliyah and enlist in the Israeli Defense Forces. He sent enthusiastic letters full of descriptions of the splendid state, the "land of milk and honey." During the War of Independence, Shimon fought in the battle for Ramleh, which is where he settled. After a year of missing their son, Itzhak's parents decided to make Aliyah with the rest of the kids at a time when the country had only celebrated a year of independence and was embroiled in daily struggles for survival. Grandpa Eli refused to make Aliyah. He said all that talk about the land of milk and honey was rubbish, that it was a country with far too many problems to live a good life. After receiving a permit to immigrate to America, he took the rest of his children and their children with him. They all sailed to Brooklyn, and Tzipke's family did the same. First, they stopped in Canada, and later arrived in the "land of endless possibilities." There, they were initially hosted by family members who had escaped Poland before the war, immigrating to America in the 1930s, before the Nazis had bared their claws to tear apart the meat of their family. Numerous relatives did not survive the war. Tzipke didn't forget her Ichu but was sure he had long since forgotten her. At the same time, Ichu was unable to find her, which made their promised marriage and imagined family together impossible. But here they were, together again.

I, having had the honor of bringing the two back together and telling their story, organized a special evening for the families. The plan was to give each of them a copy of their family story, discuss the contents, and celebrate the present moment together—most importantly, the wonderful surprises of life, which are never to be taken for granted, and which can be wildly unexpected.

Last summer, at the age of eighty-six, blind, deaf, and sick with cancer, Itzhak took a trip with the love of his youth, teenage years, and old age, a woman of eighty-five years, along with their children and grandchildren, to the village where they were born, to uncover a slice of their childhood. It was hard to recognize the place, which had since become a city, and where Jews no longer lived. There was not even a trace of the Jewish community that had once thrived in Tarnobrzeg before the war. They traveled through the big cities, visited the concentration camps where their family members had perished, and when they returned to Israel, they both said, with laughter on their lips, that they now knew better than ever that nothing was certain in this world.

I agreed with them, and at the same time, I have to offer an amendment: Even if nothing is certain, there are some things we can always depend on. Tzipke and Itzhak's love, for example, is eternal; my love for my family is eternal; and I know that Yairi's and my relationship, with all its ups and downs, despite and because of everything, is steadfast. I know that renovating the house, making the living room smaller and closing off a room just for me, will be a huge help for all the life stories I'll continue to write, and the stories I'll write hatched from my own mind. I picked out a plush red armchair and an antique desk for my computer, right by a window that looks out on the old strawberry bush that's been growing in our garden for years. A small rug will grace the floor, and landscapes, family photographs from our trip to Holland, and a small drawing I made a few years ago will line the walls.

Chapter Sixty-Seven: ICHU, MAY 1948

LEAVING GERMANY

The number of residents in the DP camp dwindled over the months. Every day, at least a few families set off, some of them for America to unite with family members, others disappeared quietly, without saying where. Father said those families have their sights set on illegal immigration to Palestine. The Jewish State of Israel declared its independence the previous week, and since then, Mother and Father have been worried sick. Shimon is fighting in the war that has been raging since the declaration, and we haven't received any news from him in a while. When I told my parents that I was really worried for Shimon's safety, they assured me that knowing Shimon, he would find a way to get by, wherever he was.

Tzipke's parents told my parents that they had decided to leave for America, but they didn't tell me anything. I guess they knew I wouldn't take it too easily, and that it was up to Tzipke to be the bearer of the bad news. Tzipke ended up telling me their family was immigrating to Brooklyn the following week, and she didn't know when we'd ever see each other again. She cried, while I hugged her and said that nothing would ever come between us, not even the entire distance from Germany to America, but deep inside I knew that it would be awfully difficult to keep in touch, given the complicated circumstances. Even though my parents could also have gone to America, they decided to make Aliyah to Israel, to join Shimon as soon as possible.

The day finally came for Tzipke's family to leave. As we were about to say goodbye, I placed the coin that had accompanied and protected me through all the war years in Tzipke's hands. I told her that it would keep her safe, and by doing so, I would be safe, too, and I reiterated my promise that we would get married someday. Sniffling through her tears, she vowed to wait for me, to never love anybody else, and I swore that I wouldn't either, adding that the heart couldn't fight its devotion. In America, Tzipke would learn to read, write, and speak in English, so I would do the same, but until then, I told her, we would write letters in the Holy tongue we'd learned in the DP camp. She smiled, promising to study hard, and to take care of herself.

The parents exchanged warm hugs, and so did all the kids, and in a flash, they had walked out of the camp until I couldn't see Tzipke anymore. Mother squeezed my shoulder and said that we would leave the camp ourselves soon enough, that everything would be okay, and that's really what happened.

We waited for months to receive notice of our Aliyah permit. Finally, in March 1949, we were told our turn had come. The activists stopped by, and we packed up everything we had, which still wasn't much—just a few articles of clothing, shoes, and souvenirs from the DP camp. When we left the camp, we also said goodbye to my grandpa, who set out with my aunts—the ones who were left—and my cousins for Brooklyn shortly afterward.

Grandpa had refused to make Aliyah under any circumstances.

I heard him saying loud and clear to Mother that "Israel will always be unsafe, an unstable land of conflict." I didn't quite understand what he meant, but Mother replied that she would go wherever Shimon went—wherever he decided to pledge his allegiance in war, fighting for the Jewish state with all his might—there, she would stay. Her family would not be torn apart. Mother put her foot down, and Grandpa understood that while he had won many other battles, he would have to give up on this one, difficult though it was. Grandpa respected my parents' decision to make Aliyah. He told my mother he loved her and that he hoped we would all be very happy.

On the day we left the camp, I asked Grandpa to tell Tzipke, whenever he found her family, that I hadn't received a letter from her. I asked him to send me her address to Israel so that I could write to her myself. Grandpa hugged me and promised that it would be "one of the first things I'll do when I get to America." Hugging him back, I said that he was the best grandpa in the world, that I would miss him terribly, and then he asked me to keep the tefillin he'd given me on my bar mitzvah safe, and I promised I would, always. Tears fell from Grandpa's eyes as he hugged me, and his hands, even though he was old, were just as strong as they had been when I was a little boy. When Grandpa hugged me, I burst into tears, not knowing when I'd see him again, if ever, since Grandpa could disappear just like Tzipke had, swallowed into a black hole.

The messengers who came to pick us up rushed us out of the camp, onto a Romanian ship that was waiting for us. From there, it would take a few days to arrive in the Jewish state, which would become our country, from which nobody would ever be able to kick us out or tell us what "stinky Jews" we were.

We boarded the ship on a sunny day. Everybody got seasick, and near Crete, a storm rocked the waters violently, but I was happy to be on such a journey, happy to be on my way to my new country, excited for the moment I would see Shimon, who promised to be waiting for us at the port. When I saw the Land of Israel from a distance, I heard Father hollering into the sky, "*Sheyichianu vekiyemanu vehigiyanu lazman haze.*"

Chapter Sixty-Eight: MAYA, 2020

TEL AVIV

The big day was upon us. The book was finished; the presentation prepared. At the entrance to the nursing home, which was situated in the shade of a tree-lined boulevard, was a fancy table piled with books. The story of one special man who had just celebrated his eighty-seventh birthday was spread across pages upon pages with old family photographs thrown in here and there to enliven the text. On the first page, there was a dedication, which I took from Itzhak's own mouth: "Dedicated with love to those who survived, those who were lost, those who emerged broken, and those who did not allow the hardship of the years to break their spirit. To optimism, the love of man, the love of life. The book is also dedicated to my beloved children, grandchildren, great-grandchildren, to everyone who passed through my life, and to those who still do today."

Slowly, the lounge in Itzhak and Tzipke's nursing home filled up with acquaintances old and new, family members, friends from all walks of life, everybody crowded together; even Itzhak's elderly cousin, his beloved Aunt Gail's daughter, had come all the way from Brooklyn accompanied by her children, grandchildren, and even a great-grandchild. Itzhak's children, grandchildren, great-grandchildren, and of course, Lior and

Matan came, as well as Yairi and Avishay, along with Dana and little Gali. We all gathered together to celebrate Itzhak's life, as well as Tzipke's, and in many ways, to celebrate the lives of all Holocaust survivors, who, despite all that they had endured, had come this far.

I opened the event by introducing our hero, saying a bit about what I'd learned during the year that I'd worked on Itzhak's family story; I spoke about Tzipke and her family; and of course, about my own family and myself. The past year of writing had changed me. I had matured, gained wisdom, learned to appreciate what I had much more than before meeting Itzhak.

The journey of Itzhak's life had become a personal journey for me. Peeling away at my unknown layers, I slowly confronted ruptures and crises I hadn't known I could handle; but with a bit of good will, empathy, and forgiveness, true forgiveness, I was able to bridge the gap and bear witness to a change within myself. I learned that growth is an individual journey, but that having good people beside you who really care about you helps a great deal. I learned that fulfilling wishes is important, too.

I stood there in front of everyone telling Itzhak's story. When I finished speaking, I asked Itzhak to say a few words. He stood up and offered his own version of the past year's journey, expressing how thankful he was for it in general, and more specifically for finding Tzipke. And then, without any warning, he pulled a ring out of his pocket, invited Tzipke to the stage, and placed the ring on her finger. The room buzzed with even more excitement and emotion; not a single eye remained dry in the room. Then Tzipke asked to say a few words. She pulled an old, rusty coin from her pocket, and with a trembling voice, said, "Itzhak, my life, I am now prepared to give back the coin you gave me to watch over so many years ago."

Presenting the coin to the audience, she continued, "This coin was on its own decades-long journey. It left a small town in Poland in 1939 for the depths of Russia, Siberia, afterward traveling through Germany to Canada and the United States, to Israel, then back to the United States, back to Israel again, and since then, it has been tucked safely away. Ichu, I took care of it just as I promised, and I know that today I can give it back to you, and in addition, leave my heart in your care. Our dream came true, even if we never believed it truly to be possible. Does it really matter how many years it took to fulfill?" Tzipke laughed. Laughing with her, we gave them both a round of applause. Itzhak hugged Tzipke close to him, saying that the coin would be under both of their watches from now on; and we all smiled and shared in their joy. At that moment, Yair gazed at me with a look of unwavering pride. Gali whispered something to him, which I overheard since she doesn't really know how to whisper: "*Aba*," she said, "isn't it true that you and Ima love each other the most in the whole world, just like Itzhak and Tzipke?" I grinned at Yairi, and he grinned right back at me.

Icho (Yitzhak) Hauser puts on the tefillin he received for his bar mitzvah from Grandpa Eli.

THANK YOU

I would like to thank my cousin Ofra Soffri for recording her father with dedication, making sure to update me every step of the way. Without you, this book would never have been written.

I would also like to thank my wonderful editor, Shlomit Lika, for her astute suggestions and for working with me. Working with you always feels like coming home.

Lastly, I thank Yad Vashem for their help in locating historical resources.

Bibliography

1. "בלטמן דניאל, "נכרים במולדתם – https://www.yadvashem.org/odot_pdf/Microsoft%20Word%20-%205154.pdf
2. בן ציון יהושע, טשקנט עיר הלחם – עקורים במלחמת העולם השנייה, אימגו, נובמבר 2007.
3. פנקס הקהילות (תשמ"ד) אנציקלופדיה של היישובים היהודיים למן היווסדם ועד לאחר שואת מלחמת העולם השנייה, פולין, כרך שלישי, יד ושם.
4. Zvi Gitelman (Editor), (1997) "Bitter Lgacy – Confronting the Holocaust in the USSR", Indiana University Press.
5. Samuel Honig (1996) "From Poland to Russia and Back", Black Moss Press.
6. P. Meyer, B.d. Weinryb, E. Duschinsky, N. Sylvan, (1953) "The Jews in the Soviet Satellites", S.U Press.
7. Arad Yitzhak, (2013) "The Holocaust in the Soviet Union, University of Nebraska Press and Yad Vashem, Jerusalem.
8. https://www.academia.edu/32677912/The_Repatriates_in_the_Displaced_Persons_Camps_1946_1947_Moreshet_97_2016_Hebrew_
9. https://encyclopedia.ushmm.org/content/en/article/heidenheim-displaced-persons-camp
10. http://holocaust.umd.umich.edu/interview.php?D=cohenr&section=74
11. http://holocaust.umd.umich.edu/

www.ingramcontent.com/pod-product-compliance
Lightning Source LLC
LaVergne TN
LVHW010313070526
838199LV00065B/5540